P9-DBK-329

In the same

INTERNATIONAL FILM GUIDE SERIES

edited by Peter Cowie

The Cinema of Orson Welles *by Peter Cowie*

Hitchcock's Films *by Robin Wood*

The Marx Brothers
Their World of Comedy *by Allen Eyles*

French Cinema since 1946
(Vol. 1: The Great Tradition
Vol. 2: The Personal Style) *by Roy Armes*

Swedish Cinema *by Peter Cowie*

The Musical Film *by Douglas McVay*

Buster Keaton *by J.-P. Lebel*

Animation in the Cinema *by Ralph Stephenson*

The Horror Film *by Ivan Butler*

The Cinema of Joseph Losey *by James Leahy*

The Western
An Illustrated Guide *by Allen Eyles*

Suspense in the Cinema *by Gordon Gow*

The Cinema of Alain Resnais *by Roy Armes*

A Dictionary of the Cinema *by Peter Graham*

4 GREAT COMEDIANS

CHAPLIN, LLOYD KEATON, LANGDON

by

DONALD W. McCAFFREY

A. ZWEMMER LIMITED, LONDON
A. S. BARNES & CO., NEW YORK

Acknowledgements

WHILE I am indebted to many people and organisations for help with this study, I would like to express my appreciation to Dr. John Kuiper, The Library of Congress, Washington D.C.; Eileen Bowser, Museum of Modern Art Film Library, New York; Dr. Donald C. Bryant, University of Iowa; the Faculty Research Committee, and Dr. William E. Koenker at the University of North Dakota. The Museum of Modern Art Film Library and Eugene Holweger are to receive thanks for the photographs which appear in this book. I am especially indebted to Harold Lloyd and the late Buster Keaton for the time given me during interviews in Hollywood, June of 1965. And to Joann, my wife, who assisted in all details of my research, I dedicate this work. Without such assistance—encouragement and financial aid—this book would not have been written.

FIRST PUBLISHED 1968

This edition prepared by The Tantivy Press
in association with A. Zwemmer Ltd.
and A. S. Barnes & Co. Inc.

Library of Congress Catalog Card Number: 68-24001

Printed in England by Page & Thomas Ltd., Chesham

Contents

Introduction

IT IS MY thesis that four comedians, Chaplin, Lloyd, Keaton, and Langdon, were the essence of that which is the best of silent screen comedy. These men, with their skills of comic story telling and acting, formulated some of the finest high-spirited comedy that has been produced in the twentieth century. How they did it and what they have created will be my theme. I will not go over old ground by providing the biographical information that can be found elsewhere, but I hope I will add a new dimension to the study of the silent screen comedy. A meticulous, shot-by-shot study of the features produced by these four comedians has been conducted. Details have been recorded more accurately by developing scenarios from the best prints of the films I could obtain; a hand-cranked editola has been one of my best tools.

While the focus is placed on major films of the Twenties which represent the four comedians' best efforts, short one- and two-reel works will also be examined to show their development. Chapters 1 and 3 will help set them in their milieu and establish a foundation for evaluating the worth of the films. By such a process I hope to initiate a specific critical approach that has often been lacking in previous writings. However, I also hope that my approach will still contain some of the appreciation of the comedy film stimulated by earlier writers.

The numbers that appear with the quotations and elsewhere in the text correspond to those in the bibliography at the back of the book.

1. In the Beginning, Mack Sennett...

HE SAT in his rocking chair. When a slight creaking was heard in the dark chamber where heads focused on flickerings of light and shadow, the film had potentialities; when a strong, rapid pulsation of noise from the rocker followed the wild action on the screen, the little two-reeler was bound to be a success. The rocking chair winner was Mack Sennett, self-styled "King of Comedy" or, as Gene Fowler called him, "Father Goose." This celluloid comedy pioneer was the entrepreneur who launched reels of laughter into the remote parts of this country and the world in the early part of the century. Crude and often naive, his raucous films brought happiness to many people and weaned a host of comedy stars such as Charles Chaplin, Marie Dressler, Edgar Kennedy, Charlie Chase, Mabel Normand, Harry Langdon, Charlie Murray, Ford Sterling, Slim Summerfield, and Ben Turpin. Few of these stars remained with his company, but they got a toe hold in the motion picture world, learned the art of slapstick, and moved on to other film-makers to disperse their talents in and for an age that thrived on laughter and joy.

The labour and birth of silent screen comedy could be chronicled with many conjectures and the positing of many views on the contributions that made this lively film form a full fledged *enfant terrible* of the arts. Some historians discover its origin springs from the primitive horseplay of the laboratory scientists (who produced burlesque skits before crude cameras) or find this genre evolving from the fertile, whimsical, theatrically oriented little farces of Méliès. Other speculators may place the emphasis on the embryonic comic films of the Italian and

English "trick films".* Furthermore, a film scholar may search out the efforts of the early vaudeville comedian's routine before the camera and see this comedy "turn" as a strong contribution to the growth of the comic film.

After an apprenticeship as an actor with D. W. Griffith and a comedy director for Biograph, Sennett became the fountainhead for the comic film in the 1910's. When he decided to produce his own comedies, he formed his own comedy troupe with the backing of Adam Kessel and Charles Baumann. One of his earliest Keystone Company products, *Cohen at Coney Island*, a one-reel work, was released on September 23, 1912, featuring comedians Ford Sterling, Mabel Normand, and Fred Mace. Writer, director, and actor, totally involved in his works, Sennett existed a world apart from the genteel, theatrical comedies of John Bunny, one of the first comedy stars of motion pictures. Also, Sennett's comedy was a world apart from the light comedy of Mary Pickford, Douglas Fairbanks, and the team, Mr. and Mrs. Sidney Drew. These actors embraced the genteel tradition, with very small dashes of slapstick. With Sennett, on the other hand, the spice became the pudding. His works had all the wild antics of the chase and trick films of the early French and Italian producers. But Sennett developed his own brand of slapstick. He often burlesqued the serious films of his day, and in doing so, evolved a type of comic film which established a tradition.

The recipe for the Sennett comic pudding was essentially simple and straightforward. His Keystone films brewed up a *pot-pourri* of broad physical actions: fights, chases, accidental falls, relentless pursuits, and bungled rescues. Keystone

*John Montgomery's first chapter in *Comedy Films*[19] does a commendable job of examining some of these early efforts.

peopled its one- and two-reel comic world with caricatures; the fat, the skinny, the rich, the poor, the stupid, the pompous, the shy, the aggressive. These cartoon-like portraits became embroiled in misunderstandings, misrepresentations, meaningless altercations, and even clandestine affairs. The plotting of the little farces sprang from material as uncomplicated as a *commedia dell' arte* scenario of the 17th century. One quality dominated the films—a nose-thumbing, anti-sentimental treatment of character and situation.

Sennett overrated the significance of his comic pokes at authority by declaring that when his comedians kicked a policeman or a society matron "the common people took a lick at all the upstarts, or intrenched, or pretentious people . . . the downfall of pretension runs through most great comic works, emphatically including Shakespeare."[24] Such a justification for slapstick comedy seems in itself pretentious. Nevertheless, Sennett's lusty comedy did not depend on his application of comic theory. It just *was*. It did not have time to follow rules. Fortunately it did not have the saccharine politeness of much of the light comedy of the time; such works cleared a pathway for a more lively, honest comedy that was to follow.

Many of Sennett's works were burlesques of serious films, novels, and events of the times. For example, the climactic fight and chase sequences were embraced by serious filmmakers in the 1910's and 1920's. It took a man like Sennett to lampoon the excesses in the treatment of such material. The heroic and sentimental poses of the protagonists of the popular fiction of the time needed deflation. The irreverent kick on the rump which Sennett directed at many *mores* of the times provoked a cool, refreshing breeze in the world of popular entertainment.

With great drive and the obsession of a Fuller Brush salesman, Sennett established a comedy mill that turned out a mass produced product. As many as nineteen comedies were in various stages of completion at one time, a production procedure that parallels, in a sense, today's method of creating films for television series. As with many mass produced items, there was a shortage of quality. The strange fruit of Sennett's mill was ground out—one-reel comedies were thrown together in a week or even in a few days; the six-reel feature, *Tillie's Punctured Romance* (1915), was shot in forty days according to Sennett's recollection.[24]

The self-named "King of Comedy" was an enterprising producer who by personality and design could only loosely be called a creator. He was more of a manager or ringmaster and, at best, an entrepreneur. He gathered a battery of actors, acrobats, animals, gag writers, and directors to his bosom. True, he supervised the handling of the story material for practically all of his films, but it would be difficult to determine how much credit he can be given for a raucous film genre of which he has been called "creator." The contributions of others, such as Hal Roach and Al Christie, should not be overlooked. These men and others, chiefly the four great cinema comedians, Chaplin, Lloyd, Keaton, and Langdon, were to develop that genre which Sennett promoted with all his considerable energy and dogged effort.

A taskmaster with a giant ego, Sennett ruled his kingdom with all the authority he could muster. To his odd collection of low-brow clowns and hack writers he was just short of being a slave driver. According to biographer Gene Fowler, he did not like to argue or be contradicted. He could only be swayed from his view if the speaker made it "painless and indirect."[9]

Sennett's explanation of his attitude toward his company was somewhat similar to Fowler's, but naturally, he appeared to have a stronger sense of humour, a good natured demeanour toward his crew in the autobiographical work, *King of Comedy*. Although he could conceivably display tyrannical traits and still be able to produce a quality product or service, Sennett's greatest weakness was probably his distorted demand of loyalty from his staff. He also resisted giving higher positions and raises in salary even to the comedians who developed into strong box-office attractions. Chaplin was a prime example.

In his recent autobiography Chaplin indicates that he was not always on good terms with Sennett because he was considered to be a difficult person to work with, and the self-styled "King of Comedy" told the comedian, " 'Just do what you're told and we'll be satisfied.' "[6] The comedian explains that his desire to write and direct did not sit well with Sennett, and he was "assigned to Mabel Normand" because she seemed to have the charm to handle him. But even this arrangement would not work. Chaplin claims that he had to promise Sennett the money ($1500) lost in making the film if his first directing assignment were not successful.[6] Chaplin claims that only the growing success of his films kept him from being fired. Of course, two strong egos were clashing in this situation. Sooner or later there would have to be a parting of the way.

> Now: the rumour runs, and all motion-picture histories that I have examined say that I let Charlie Chaplin go because I did not appreciate him enough to pay him the money he deserved. The fact was this: When $750 was not enough I asked Chaplin what salary he thought would be right. He declined to mention a sum. I then made a decision on the spot

> and offered Charlie Chaplin half my kingdom. I mean precisely that. I owned one third of the Keystone studio (soon to become the Mack Sennett Studio) and I offered to split my share with Chaplin if he would stay with us. That is to say, my tender to Chaplin was one sixth of Keystone. When he turned that down I had no more chips to raise the bet with.[24]

As fair as this might seem to some—if we can trust Sennett's recollection—it can still be concluded that Sennett was penny-wise and pound-foolish. Many other accounts of his attempt to keep down salaries of his leading actors have been reported. The fact remains that he lost many of his best comedians to producers who would pay them more money. True, not all of them became stars, although Chaplin, Lloyd, and Langdon left his company to become the leaders in the field. Keaton, however, never worked for Sennett.

Witness Fowler's account of a row when Hampton Del Ruth, his scenario editor, left him:

> . . . Sennett climbed out of his bath, dressed, and went roaring through the lot, shouting defiantly: "Quit! All of you. I can get up my own stories, build my own sets, photograph and direct my own pictures, and act the lead in them, too. Quit and be damned!"[9]

Certainly this was a man of explosive, egocentric temperament. While such a disposition shows the wild extent of the energy and ego which established a productive company in the 1910's, it also shows the weakness. Furthermore, such behaviour would lead to a type of rigidity—a stubbornness that pits itself against change—that eventually would make a Sennett film sterile. Time would catch up with him. His disposition was suitable for a pioneer but not a perfector. Certainly, Sennett had a basic honesty—a kind of crude integrity that made his early works vital stepping stones to films that would reach greater heights. But the quality of originality was often lacking. Even he, who had been credited with many innovations, admitted in one of his more humble moments that he borrowed heavily. He wrote:

> Now, I have been posing for many years as the inventor of slapstick motion-picture comedy and it is about time I confessed the truth. It was those Frenchmen who invented slapstick and I imitated them. I never went as *far* as they did, because give a Frenchman a chance to be funny and he will go the limit—you know what I mean. But I stole my first ideas from the Pathés.[24]

But this is an oversimplification; Sennett borrowed from sources besides the Pathés. He did so in a way that cannot be condemned. It was the practice of the day, and of course, no one had a copyright on basic situations and gags that had been handed down through the history of the comic drama. He can only be criticised for his weak adaptation of such materials. In a given situation he seldom seemed to display innovation—a switch in the use of an old device as it is employed with contemporary story material. Despite this shortcoming, Sennett's work had a basic honesty because it burlesqued the traditions of the day.

The exact nature of Sennett's films can be seen by comparing one of his works with John Bunny's *A Cure for Pokeritis*, a 1912 one-reel comedy replete with gentility. While Bunny's development of a comic character and his skill in acting may be applauded, the story and comic invention of his film are trite, laboured, and superficially sentimental. The humour of this work leans heavily on the minor foibles of a husband who is addicted to card playing. The husband's attempts to outwit his wife in order to carry on his vice are thwarted when a kindly young man called Cousin Freddie gets his Bible class to imitate policemen and raid the poker playing den of erring husbands. Since the wives of the offenders are a part of this conspiracy, they stage a feigned rescue after their husbands are collared by Freddie's mock police force. The "sinners" are grateful and repent as the last scene of the film fades to black. By today's standards, this work is so bland that it scarcely produces a flicker of a smile from a viewer. It is slow moving and theatrically oriented. The humorous situations obviously reflect an age in the grips of Victorian codes of behaviour. At best, the film could be designated as a polite poke at such standards; but, there seems to be a half-caress in the jab—sentiment produces creampuff humour.

In sharp contrast, Sennett's *Barney Oldfield's Race for a Life*, made only a year later in 1913, is a lively, humorous work far removed from the comedies of the genteel tradition. This one-reel film employs three times as many shots as Bunny's 1912 work and uses a fast paced comic rescue scene for its closing episode. It burlesques the melodrama, especially the type produced by the Eclectic Company which in 1913 turned out works with such excessive titles as *Doom of the Ocean*, *Fatal Plunge*, *Message of the Dead*, *His Fateful Passion*, and *Toils of Villainy*: later, in 1914, this company produced the famous serial *The Perils of Pauline*, starring Pearl White. Sennett's take-off of such works has many crude, stock devices of burlesque, but the film cannot be accused of dullness. The acting is artless even for this formative age of cinema when actors in serious films often aped the broad style of the stage. Ford Sterling as the comic villain struts and hops around as if he were playing to a theatre audience of four thousand. Mack Sennett as the country bumpkin who loves the heroine (played by Mabel Normand) slips in and out of character with each changing of locality and situation. Nevertheless, there is a broad, child-like spirit of fun that lifts this work above the polished, well-acted efforts of *A Cure for Pokeritis.* Action is cinematic—the actors move in depth, toward and away from the camera; the editing of the rescue scene assists the pace greatly. Three parallel actions are skilfully blended in this chase; the villain is shown trying to kill the heroine; the rescuers, Barney Oldfield and the comic oaf (Sennett's character), speed in a racer; and the embryonic Keystone Cops struggle with a railroad handcar to get to the scene of the assault.

Interestingly enough, Sennett's fresh, vivacious comedy may have achieved many of these cinematic techniques because of the method he used to shoot his films. He often filmed his early works without the benefit of elaborate sets and costumes. But his movies developed a liveliness that can be found in a spirited, devil-may-care amateur who decides to establish a little theatre or shoot a movie on a shoe string.

A look at a later work, *Tillie's Punctured Romance* (1915) reveals even more characteristics of the Sennett movie. This work gave the comedy prestige in an age of one- and two-reelers by extending the film to the unheard of length of six reels. This film might be called a prototype for many feature comedy works. A detailed examination of this movie, therefore,

Genteel comedy: John Bunny and Flora Fitch in the 1912 A CURE FOR POKERITIS.

Slapstick comedy: Mabel Normand chained to the track with Ford Sterling holding the sledge hammer in BARNEY OLDFIELD'S RACE FOR A LIFE (1913).

The broad comed of Ford Sterling, shown here as chief of the Keystone Cops, dominated the the screen until Chaplin became the leading comedian.

The first feature length comedy is considered to be TILLIE'S PUNCTURED ROMANCE, a six-reel work produced in 1915 becomes an important springboard for this study of the leading clowns of the silent screen comedy.*

Freely adapted from Marie Dressler's successful musical comedy, *Tillie's Nightmare*, Mack Sennett's movie version is a burlesque of the Cinderella story. It contains much-used plot elements from the stage and popular literature of the times. A crafty dandy lures an innocent country girl to the big city, rejects her after he has stolen her money, and rushes back to marry her when he hears she has inherited a fortune. During the 19th century such material would be treated sentimentally in the popular stage melodrama. Sennett's treatment, however, is anti-sentimental, although it retains some of the intrigue of such a plot line to hold the interest of the audience.

At the outset of the film, the burlesque treatment can be readily realised by the establishment of the comic characters. The City Slicker, a comic villain played by Charles Chaplin,† is diminutive in size and cunning; he strikes seedy, flamboyant

*Any analysis of *Tillie's Punctured Romance* runs into the problem of print validity. Many reruns and reedited versions of this highly popular feature have taken a toll. The film has been shortened to five reels and the titles have been altered. Available prints, however, all have the same lively characteristics of the original.

†This film helped in some measure to establish Chaplin's stardom. Everyone connected with the film, therefore, tries to take credit for his "discovery." Marie Dressler wrote of her decision to do the film: "When I finally agreed, I went up on the lot and looked around till I found Charlie Chaplin, who was then unknown. I picked him out and also Mabel Normand, to whom I had taken a fancy, and started in to make the picture. . . ."[47] Miss Dressler's analysis of the status of Chaplin's work in the films at this time is a distortion. He had achieved success in his one- and two-reel comedies and was on his way to stardom. *Tillie's Punctured Romance* was a vehicle that might be said to have given him another push toward the popularity that soon surpassed that of stars who played in serious films.

2

poses as he tries to charm the ladies. The victim of his scheme, Tillie, a farmer's daughter (played by Marie Dressler), is the antithesis of the sweet, charming country maid. The character is not shy, but a horse of a woman who walks over clods in the field like a waddling bear. When she is wooed, her affectionate touches are as gentle as the rabbit punch of a lady wrestler. Other personalities in this early portion of the film are bucolic caricatures from vaudeville of the 1910's and the late 19th century stage comedy.

The plot is unified by a triangle situation that results in a rivalry between the City Slicker's girl friend and Tillie—a complication that develops in the second sequence of the film when the comic villain lures Tillie to the city. This conflict continues until the resolution of the film; the dandy is rejected and the two rivals become warm friends.

Above all, the meat of this prototype of the feature length comic film lies in a whole gamut of slapstick. Most noticeable in the early sequences of the film is the broad physical humour of abuse. Brickbats fly through the air, thrown intentionally or accidentally, and send the victim sprawling. Minor insults promote a cuff to the side of the face or the jaw; and kicks on the rump abound. More cleverly motivated than such stock comedy producing devices, Tillie's gesticulations account for some of the best slapstick. When she waves her arms to express her joy, one of her hands inevitably hits the end of the City Slicker's nose. Crude as it may seem, Tillie often produces a swing of her hips that strikes the little man and sends him teetering and crumpling to the ground. Affectionately, the country maid tosses a bouquet of flowers in the dandy's face with enough force to bowl him over; he smiles tightly and counters with a brickbat which evidently hurts but barely moves her bulk.

In the second sequence of the film, Tillie gets drunk in a restaurant and creates a grotesque spectacle as she is taken to the police station. She tries to dance with her escorting policeman and joyfully, affectionately slaps him. In the jail she bites the chief of police's finger.

Physical indignities are heaped upon the servants of Tillie's inherited mansion in sequence four of the work. In one of the longer, sustained pantomime routines of the film, Chaplin's genius in portraying the crudities of the *nouveau riche* produces a sparkling scene. A detailed quote from a scenario which I've prepared in the study of this film will best illustrate how rich with insult humour this work becomes:

> 246 LS*—Charlie and Tillie walk into the plush room of the mansion from the background left. Servants stand at attention right and left, showing the new owners the way. One servant, on the left side—where Charlie stops—extends his arm. Charlie hangs his cane on the outstretched arm and places his hat in the servant's hand. Tillie points out that the other servant has nothing. Charlie gives him the hat and then leans back on the servant's chest. He then turns to this man and blows smoke from his cigarette into his face. He takes out the servant's lapel handkerchief and blows his nose on it—returns it by draping it over his hand. Charlie leans his elbow on the chest of the servant, crosses his legs nonchalantly, and listens to Tillie talk. Tillie

*The number 246 is the shot number (LS meaning long-shot) I use as a reference point in the film which I have in my private library. I use the name "Charlie" for the character of the City Slicker because Chaplin often uses his first name in his films. This film, however, does not use a specific identification of the character except in the opening cast of characters title when the label "City Slicker" appears.

> leans against the other servant's chest—the one on the right. Again Charlie blows smoke in the servant's face; the servant sneezes; Charlie glares at him. Tillie comes over to this "offending" servant and slaps his face. Then for no particular reason at all, she goes to the servant on the right and gives him a short jab to the chin with the palm of her hand. . . .

A variation on such slapstick of abuse is used in sequence five. Much of the comedy focuses on the bungled attempts of Tillie and her husband to become society lions. Drinking too much punch, they try imitating the dance steps of two professional entertainers who have been hired for their party. Tillie drags her husband about the dance floor and dances with a vigour that sends Charlie twirling into a dizzy collapse.

Sequence six, the last one of the film, shows characteristics of the final portion of the two-reel comedies of the time. Fight and chase situations compose the material for this lively sequence. A rich gentleman, Mr. Woozis (played by Chester Conklin), and Charlie get into a "knock-'em-down-and-drag-'em-out" fight. The "little tramp", slightly tipsy from too much punch, puts his right foot on the gentleman's lap—an act which incites the wild fight. Charlie is the victor of the combat because of the energy of his dogged assault and the deft French kicks which he places soundly on Mr. Woozis's chest. The ease and mock dignity with which Chaplin executes his dance-like moves show excellent use of knockabout comedy. Clearly, such pantomime illustrates Chaplin's training in the music hall stages of London.

Far more cinematic in treatment, the final chase portion of the film shows Charlie and his girl friend, Mabel, being pursued by a wild-eyed, furious Tillie who blazes away at them with a pistol. Bungling policemen rush to the scene of the altercation.

Typical frantic actions of the Keystone Cops fill the screen with a madcap rush and tumble. Sennett shows the running policemen bumping into pedestrians, falling from a speeding, open-topped automobile, and driving their car crazily down the street. The car finds its mark and knocks Tillie off a pier into the ocean. Then, the would-be rescuers have the driver of the vehicle back away from the accident, but argue over the wheel so vehemently that the automobile weaves to the end of the pier again and plunges into the water. More police arrive and after three blundering attempts to lift the elephantine Tillie from the ocean (where she is fighting off crabs and fish), they finally rescue the weary, water-logged comic heroine.

In all, *Tillie's Punctured Romance* has many crudities, not only in primitive humour, but also in the acting and the technical use of the medium. Marie Dressler's acting is broad to the point of over-acting; Chaplin, although he has some effective moments, is caught up in a whirlwind pace that makes him appear only slightly more talented than the run-of-the-mill Keystone comedian. Often pantomimed intentions of a character are overdone. There is some crude finger-pointing by both Dressler and Chaplin to convey such information as "You must go with me this way"—a statement conveyed by the character pointing to himself, to the other person, and to the direction he wishes to go. When Tillie decides she will become a waitress in the big city, Dressler faces the camera lens squarely, gestures as if she were holding a tray, and points to a nearby café.

Camera shots and editing are often as primitive as the comedy. Poor framing of the subjects is often present, and few close-ups are used to convey necessary information, let alone point up a gag. A goodly share of mismatched shots during a character's movements from place to place also occur in the film; and the establishment of locale is often fuzzy. Curiously enough, the final chase sequence seems far advanced of its time. It contains many shots of short duration which match (and enhance) the speed of the action. The variety of shot angles used is extensive. Parallel actions are blended into an excellent mosaic of comic situation. There is a madness in the logic of the editing of such materials—but there is method in it. Evidently Sennett's flair for editing a chase sequence had become quite sophisticated by this time.

The passing of a few years was to reveal weaknesses in Sennett's films. His greatest shortcoming seemed to be in his inflexible theory and working methods which did not change with the times. In 1926 his *A Sea Dog's Tale*, starring Billy Bevan, appeared to be a product of 1915 vintage. The material given to the comedian was trite and contrived. The final underwater scenes of the film seemed to be pirated from an underwater sequence that Buster Keaton rejected from his *The Navigator* (1924) because it was contrived and didn't follow the action of the story. Sennett was obviously using old slapstick devices without seeking fresh twists on his material. One stock device followed another without allowing the comic character to assist in the development of the gags. In the Twenties Sennett was adhering to the theory of writing that he had developed early in his career. He believed that "events are piled on too rapidly" to develop character in comedy.[70] Consequently, his practice of using stock devices without some degree of character development dated his works in the Twenties and certainly accounts for their inferiority to some of the other works of the period.

In his *World of Laughter* Kalton C. Lahue holds the view that Sennett changed with the times in the Twenties.[16] My research and observation of films lead me to the opposite view. Hal Roach's Laurel and Hardy two-reelers in the late Twenties are certainly superior to any Sennett work of the time. Lahue states, in one of his rare qualifications, that Sennett had lost much of his old comedy flavour but still "retained his deft touch for selecting funny subject matter, and several of the gems of silent screen parody came from this time."[16]

Unfortunately, Lahue is not clear in this somewhat extensive (rather than intensive) view of what he calls the "motion picture comedy short from 1910 to 1930," and he does not include supporting material to sustain his views. He makes a further error in his elevation of the comedy pioneer by writing, "With the exception of Chaplin, no comedian who left Sennett ever attained greater fame than he had while with him."[16] Lloyd, of course, is the most notable "exception" he overlooks, and Harry Langdon reached the peak of his stardom in features directed by Frank Capra.

Such lapses by Lahue are not as important as his overrating of Sennett. Hal Roach had adapted with the times; his two-reelers with Charlie Chase were superior to a Sennett product of the Twenties. The 1926 *When a Man's a Prince* with Ben Turpin was a crude burlesque of the romantic, serious movie of the age. While Roach had many weak films, such Charlie Chase works as *Long Live the King*, made the same year, were superior burlesques when compared with Sennett's.

It should also be remembered that Roach was producer of Harold Lloyd's *Grandma's Boy* (1922) and *Safety Last* (1923). Sennett's early Twenties features such as *A Small Town Idol* (a 1921 work starring Ben Turpin) suffer greatly when compared with Lloyd's full length films.

I agree with Seldes when he states that a Keystone product

often "lacked variety, it was often dull, its lapses of taste were serious . . ." and it was "a fairly standardised article."[23] Seldom did the material change from film to film—only the comedian was different and only his treatment of the material, when he was allowed individuality, seemed to create a degree of variety.

Despite his faults, Sennett established the formula for producing the film comedy. He discovered that it was most effective to have a battery of gag writers working on a film, and he found that certain kinds of material could be handled by specific comedians. Most important of all, Sennett left his trademark on the comic film by the direction which he gave it. His *Tillie's Punctured Romance* was a blueprint for the feature comedy film. True, it was a crude plan that had many structural defects. It seemed to be an elongation of the two- or three-reel film. But it was a start. This first feature length comedy film established a story-telling method that was to influence some of the best comic features of the 1920's. Sennett can also be credited with the exploration of almost all the comic possibilities which others would later employ and embellish. The major comedians who were to spring from this crude but colourful and lively slapstick tradition had the pioneer, Mack Sennett, to set up the signposts for them.

2. Enter from the Background— A Lost Soul

FORTUNATELY Charles Chaplin was gradually able to break away from the format of the Sennett comic film. While the famous comedian owed much to the Sennett tradition—the story material and plotting, the techniques of the medium, and the comic vigour—he had his own contribution to make to the comic film. The more subtle comedy of this English music hall entertainer was thwarted by the fast pace and farcical plotting of the Sennett one- and two-reel comedy. While Chaplin's performance in *Tillie's Punctured Romance* brought him renown in the pre-World War I era, it is not likely that his fame would have lasted if he had never progressed beyond this work. Modern critics would merely have judged the actor as a competent, above average comedian of the formative days of the silent screen comedy. Instead, critics of our age have praised Chaplin more than any comedian of our century. Theodore Huff writes that he is "a clown in direct descent from the *commedia dell' arte* . . . the twentieth century counterpart of Arlequin and Grimaldi . . . a symbol of the age, the twentieth-century Everyman."[11] Peter Cotes and Thelma Niklaus declare: "He and Dickens are of the same stock, filled with the same humanism, the same passionate pity for the underdog, the same blaze of anger against persecution, exploitation, and injustice."[7] Robert Payne becomes even more rhapsodic:

> Far more than Sir Galahad, he represents the heroic figure of the man pure and undefiled, and he is all the more credible because he is reduced to a human scale. . . . Charlie emerges as the knight-errant of the back streets, the knight of faith, the devout tight-rope walker who, simply by maintaining his balance on the tight-rope, holds the circus tent and everyone in it from falling into a bottomless abyss.[21]

Strong words! Nonsense? When examined unemotionally, a

sober, detached evaluator might reject such 1950 observations as just short of nonsense. It is easy to become rhapsodic after being captured by the charm of this comedian. Chaplin's works are emotionally charged and provoke such responses. As an antiquarian in love with silent screen comedy, I am naturally enthusiastic myself. I believe, however, he has been overrated at the expense of his contemporaries, Harold Lloyd, Buster Keaton, and Harry Langdon. I find much in Chaplin that makes him the greatest clown of our age, but not the Everyman, or the Sir Galahad. There is a profundity in the tramp—a dimension that places him on a high plane; yet I believe that many critics attribute qualities to him that go beyond the province of the clown. Granted, many of these comments make interesting reading (and may give their author the label of a penetrating critic with intellectual insights that soar above the commonplace. After all, why write about that which is easily detected?), but such views are often limited, impressionistic, and too individualistic, even though they may promote appreciation for the art they applaud. On the other hand, the drama of the comedian is usually underrated or even dismissed as something entertaining and consequently of little significance. Therefore, I take a qualified stand. The clown may touch upon the profundities of life, but this is an added dimension. Primarily, this little fellow who is dancing in the wind, thumbing his nose, or embracing the good things of life, is concerned with the pleasure of laughter which he promotes. He is, in short, an entertainer; a bearer of happiness. It is not necessary to excuse him, to apologise for him, to elevate him. As if making us laugh were of little significance!

Probably Chaplin's greatest strength, an intense emotional involvement in his films—both in the composition and execution of the work, has inclined evaluators to write subjectively on this twentieth-century comedian. But this virtue sometimes became his fault. His films were positively and negatively affected by his strong personal traits. A look at his writings reveals the unique nature of this artist.

Three autobiographical works that Chaplin has published indicate these facets of character. The romantic-sentimental tone of his writing is striking—a strong ego shines forth in the incidents he selects and his style of writing. He overdramatises his youth in one of his first autobiographies, *My Own Story*, a rather embarrassing, lushly written work published in 1916. His early fourth-rate music hall days as a clog dancer and child comedian are told with details that seem to be drawn from a Dickens novel. Of his experiences with a manager of an all child troupe, he writes of incidents that characterise the man as cruel and perverted as Fagin. Indeed, it would seem that Chaplin as a child was living the life of Oliver Twist.

A reader who looks at *My Own Story* today will have difficulty separating fact from fiction—as Chaplin must have had in writing the work in 1916. There are moments when the sentiment is maudlin even for the age in which this autobiography was written. In his 1964 *My Autobiography*, Chaplin tones down the earlier adventures, and it would seem that some of the incidents mentioned in the 1916 account never happened. But a more sober, detached tone can be detected.

A 1922 work, *My Trip Abroad* (which reveals the comedian's affinity for the "my" in his accounts) also had the excesses of the romantic-sentimental facet in his character. As if extracted directly from his diary, he recorded his reaction to a Russian singer in the Le Raté Mort restaurant in Paris. The awkward present tense is typical of the whole work:

> She has poise, grace, and is compelling attention even in this place. There comes a bit of melancholy in the song and she sings it as one possessed, giving it drama, pathos. Suddenly there is a change. The music leaps to wild abandon. She is with it. She tosses her head like a wild Hungarian gypsy and gives fire to every note. But almost as it began, the abandon is over. With wistful sweetness, she is singing plaintively again. She is touching every human emotion in her song. At times she is tossing away care, then gently wooing, an elusive strain that is almost fairylike, that crescendos into tragedy, going into a crashing climax that diminishes into an ending, searching, yearning and wistfully sad. Her personality is written into every mood of the song. She is at once fine, courageous, pathetic and wild. She finished to an applause that reflected the indifference of the place. In spots it was spontaneous and insistent. In others little attention was paid to her. She is wasted here.[45]

While this passage indicates the romantic-sentimental temperament of Chaplin in its negative, overdrawn way, underneath the excess there are positive elements. He was obviously fascinated by many things in his environment; he had a childlike enthusiasm for people and events that others took for granted or observed with detachment and mere interest.

In this same work he revealed an unusual concern for James Barrie's negative criticism of his 1921 feature, *The Kid*:

> He is very severe. He declares that the "heaven scene was entirely unnecessary, and why did I give it so much attention? And why so much of the mother in the picture, and why the meeting of the

> mother and the father?" All of these things he is discussing analytically and profoundly, so much so that I find that my feeling of self-consciousness is rapidly leaving me.[45]

Seldom did Chaplin publicly answer or even acknowledge negative criticism of his works. He seemed to enjoy the praise and fame that greeted him—ignoring responses that would not please him. Even in his writing just cited, egocentricity was only thinly veiled. As one continues to read the above passage, he discovers that Chaplin was flattered by the attention paid him by the famous playwright—attention centring on play construction.

Part of the comedian's personality which does not at first seem linked to his art can be witnessed in *My Own Story*, his earliest fully developed writing about himself, and *My Autobiography*, his latest. He drops names readily; he seems fascinated with famous people and his association with them. Indeed, he is evidently as intrigued by renown as a *nouveau riche* who has nothing but money to make him a part of the international set. He seems more interested in his social life than his art. There is quite the opposite situation with Lloyd, Keaton, and Langdon. From all accounts I've read of their lives and works, they have been tied up in their films and the making of them to the point that only the most bland fan magazines have revealed any of the inclinations of their social awareness. To Chaplin films seem to be a strong personal expression; his attitude toward his art becomes something akin to the romantic writer's concept of inspiration—as if the whole process were something mystical that couldn't readily be analysed or discussed.

Probably Chaplin's greatest fault is linked with this attitude. To all appearances he overlooks his contemporaries and his dependence on the whole comic tradition and the milieu of his time. Chaplin's writings are about Chaplin; he rarely recognises others. I have searched in vain for accounts that reveal his views on the differences and similarities between his work and that of other comedians. These views are not public property—something put down in writing.

When I interviewed Harold Lloyd in June of 1965, I asked him about Chaplin's curious oversight—especially when I realised that both Lloyd and Keaton were so concerned with such evaluations. He told me that in private all the comedians, even Chaplin, talked over comic techniques, story construction, and specific gags from their last pictures.

It would appear that Chaplin had to promote the particular public image that he could achieve art by his genius—without perspiration and thought. Of course, accounts tell us quite the contrary. He laboured long and hard on his works. Inspiration did not come from the comic muse as a flash of light from heaven. Furthermore, Chaplin's development was nearly as slow as the other comedians'. It took many Sennett creations and many short works of his own before he reached his peak. This can be traced by looking at his formative period.

Chaplin as an entertainer (and that is how I view his greatness) began to show his acting skill and the growth of his famous comic character after he had served an apprenticeship as an actor, writer, and director with Mack Sennett. His first film as a director, *Caught in the Rain* (1914), showed little promise. It was a rather standard Sennett creation using Keystone material in both conception and execution. The dependence on farce is obvious from the plot: Charlie, as a drunken dandy, follows a married woman into a hotel and by a series of misunderstandings—namely the sleepwalking wife who comes into his room and is caught by her husband—gets thrown out the window into the rain. The robust Mack Sennett treatment clearly influenced director Chaplin. As an actor this young comedian displays his talent as a comic drunk—a skill he acquired as a famous music hall comedian in England. This one-reel film contains slapstick that is generally better motivated than the usual Keystone product. But the film is only the beginning of Chaplin's development.

After Chaplin left Sennett, he affiliated with Essanay Films, and his work showed considerable improvement. Slapstick abounded with the slow and sure evolution of the character of the little tramp. And that character was to be almost the essence of Chaplin's comedy. Sennett's formula would not allow for such character development. Even in the late Twenties, as I have pointed out, his films remained the same slapstick farces with the central comic character existing in a cartoon world of bold, sketchy, and sometimes inconsistent facets. Touches of sympathy for Chaplin's little tramp were manifested in the 1915 two-reel works *The Tramp* and *The Bank*. This added dimension provided the character facet that was the object of so many words of praise from critics who championed Chaplin's artistry.

A giant step was taken by Chaplin when he produced twelve excellently conceived and executed two-reel works for Mutual Films in 1916 and 1917. It was his most fertile period and at least one minor masterpiece, *Easy Street* (1917), sprang from this frenzy of creativity. Some of the comedian's working methods, his faults and strength came into clear focus at this time. Many of his film's plots were sketchy and erratic; such plots seemed to reflect many of the impromptu story developing techniques of the Mack Sennett tradition. *One A.M.* (1916), a *tour de force*, proved successful completely on the strength of

Chaplin's acrobatic skills and clever pantomime routines—the story line is slight. This work also shows one of the comedian's methods of gathering material. In it he incorporated material from the music hall stage. *One A.M.* is an elaborate solo routine that looks like a "turn" of a variety show merely photographed on movie film. There was little of the film that could not be as effectively presented on the stage. Only a few close-up reactions, shots of the little drunk struggling with stairs, stuffed animals, and a mechanised folding bed, showed the medium in operation. Chaplin the actor dominated. The work's main fault lay in its repetition of the pratfall (over twenty-five) and personal injury or discomfiture. Despite an attempt at variety, even Chaplin could not find enough different ways to fall and sustain the piece.

Easy Street (1917) is the one exception in the body of twelve films of this period. It is by far the best of the whole Mutual output because it has a strong dramatic story line fused with Chaplin's outstanding acting skills and ingenious gags. In this work he employed parallel plot lines with a finesse that he never completely equalled in his later efforts. Chaplin has not dipped into his background on the English stage for the routines in this film; the story is designed for the motion picture. The film has a tale that is vigorously told; it holds interest with the little fellow turned policeman and shows his conflict with a brute of a man (played broadly by Eric Campbell) and his gang of thugs. Chaplin tells his story directly and acts with economy—two virtues which are not always seen in his films. If the comedian had ceased his work for the silent screen and returned to the English music halls, he would still have a place in the sun with *Easy Street*.

Chaplin moved on and created another short, masterfully

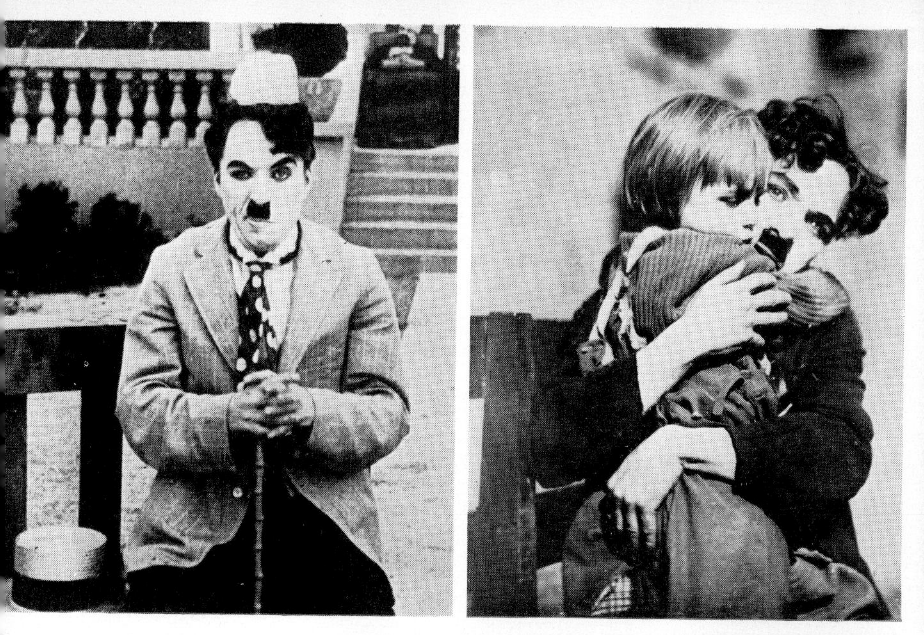

ɔove left: during his ɔst productive period, ʼhaplin created two-reel ·rks for Mutual. He is ɔwn here in the final ·ne of THE CURE ɔ17). Above right: a ıtimental reunion after ; Little Tramp has ·cefully taken "the Kid" ·m orphanage authorities THE KID (1921).

Disguised as a tree in SHOULDER ARMS (1918), the little fellow proves to be a match for the Germans.

THE GOLD RUSH (1925). This page: Chaplin as the lost soul o
the edge of society. One of his great moments of 'pathos' in the film
Opposite: hunger forces Charlie to eat his shoe, and shoestrings a
eventually devoured as if they were spaghetti (top); the little tram
teases his gold-seeking pardner as he makes advances towards a prett
young girl (below

Chaplin employs the 'thrill comedy' of Lloyd in his last feature of the Twenties, THE CIRCUS (1928).

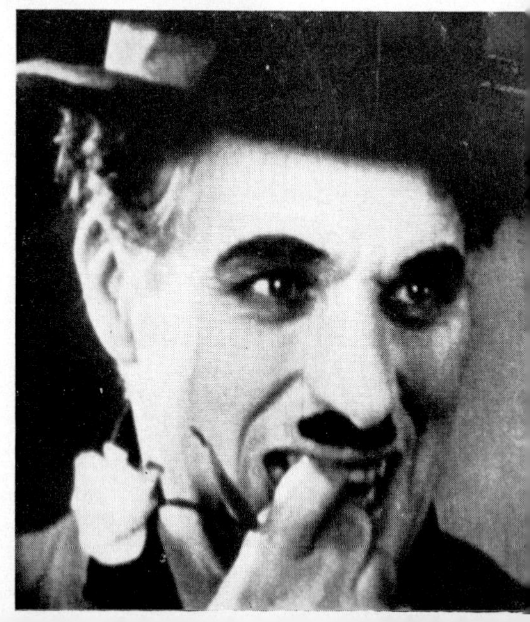

The power of the close-up and delicate acting skill are seen in the final shot of CITY LIGHTS (1931).

executed work, *Shoulder Arms*, in 1918. This excellent spoof of the trials of a doughboy of World War I is replete with well conceived comic invention. Chaplin has a brilliantly clever slapstick scene showing his little tramp disguised as a tree as he spies for U.S. forces in enemy territory. Detected by the enemy, he plays a frantic game of hide and seek with a German soldier in a wood with trees that are similar in shape to his disguise. He periodically freezes and assumes poses which match the trees around him in order to outsmart his pursuer; then he runs wildly when the soldier stabs a nearby tree with his bayonet. Full of ingenious gags, this comic chase not only outstripped Chaplin's competitor, Mack Sennett; it is a chase which can match and generally exceed in quality anything of this nature today. But the structural fault mars the work. Especially disappointing is the cliché dream ending—that is, all the exploits of the little soldier behind enemy lines are merely a figment of his nightmare.

When Chaplin started producing feature length works in 1921 with his famous *The Kid*, even more pronounced weaknesses in the dramatic story line resulted. A detailed scenario of this work reveals many structural faults. A film that uses fifteen sequences, of which the first three sequences and number fourteen have marked defects, the work has a typical crudity of story telling that Chaplin was never able to erase in his feature works. Laboriously, he begins his story with a sequence of direct, serious and (unfortunately) overdrawn, and uninspired exposition. Even banal titling encroaches on this part of the film. An unwed mother is introduced with the title "A Young Girl . . . her mistake is that she is a mother." As if under the influence of the German cinema of the time, Chaplin comments on the suffering of the young woman by interjecting a still picture of Christ bearing the cross up a hill. Throughout the first three sequences, the serious elements which Chaplin uses to sustain a feature length work are driven home with sledge-hammer blows.

In sequence fourteen, a portion of *The Kid* which is nearly six minutes long, Chaplin also mars the work by presenting an elaborate, tangential dream episode. Both damned and justified by the critics, this portion of the film received a largely negative vote. Film historians Maurice Bardèche and Robert Brasillach, for example, found this sequence a good illustration of Chaplin's tendency to insert episodes which have little bearing on the main plot.[1] Chaplin himself reports that playwright James M. Barrie found the dream portion of the film superfluous.[45]

The last sequence also mars the work. Like Chaplin's later work, *The Gold Rush* (1925), the film exhibits a forced happy ending which shows the little tramp being taken by the police to rejoin the Kid and to meet the child's mother. The swiftness of this resolution is less at fault than the trite material and the awkward handling of the situation by Chaplin. Visually (both in pantomime and camerawork) the conclusion is banal—unworthy of the amount of praise that some critics have given this short sequence. Parker Tyler, in an unusual and ridiculous symbolic analysis, sees the car that takes Charlie to the Kid and the mother as the "magic vehicle that restores order."[26] Gilbert Seldes, champion of the popular arts, misfires in his analysis of this last scene by effusively writing:

> He is ushered into a limousine instead of a patrol wagon—it is the beginning of the happy ending. And as the motor starts he flashes at the spectators of his felicity a look of indescribable poignancy. It is frightened, it is hopeful, bewildered; it lasts a fraction

> of a second and is blurred by the plate glass of the car. I cannot hope to set down the qualities of it, how it becomes a moment of unbearable intensity, and how one is breathless with suspense—and with adoration.[23]

Such a reading of this incident seems to be merely Seldes's interpolation. I have looked carefully at the action which Seldes describes and find that only a comic "take" expression of puzzlement exists on Chaplin's face. No close-up is given which would reveal the poignancy which the critic finds in this scene.

Such enthusiastic praise from the evaluators who viewed *The Kid* can be understood when the virtues of the work are set forth. My dissection of this film could not dim my feelings for the little tramp and his love for the little "orphan" that he takes under his wing. Moments of tenderness when the frail, lonely tramp embraces the Kid have all the strength and sentiment of a Dickens story brought to life. A depth of comic character that is only faintly seen in most film comedies of today is evident. Serious moments between the Kid and the little tramp illustrate the outstanding features of his films—the creation of sympathy for his characters which some critics view as the "profound" in Chaplin. Better than he had ever done before, Chaplin displayed a clown who could exhibit the slapstick of Harlequin with the moon-struck sadness of Pierrot. The fusion of these traits was not complete, however, until Chaplin had created *The Gold Rush* in 1925.

Far greater skill in story construction was exhibited by Chaplin's formidable competitor, Harold Lloyd, who created his first feature work *Grandma's Boy* in 1922, just a year after Chaplin released *The Kid*. This new work even impressed Chaplin, who was not prone to praise his rivals. The creator of the little tramp was reported to have written to Lloyd that *Grandma's Boy* was an inspiration to him to do his best work and "to be contented with nothing else but the best for himself."[19] While Lloyd's work had some weaknesses—its seventeen sequences were rather choppy in transitional phases, and the climactic fight sequence was somewhat anticlimactic after a brilliant chase scene—the film was unified by a strong central comic idea that resulted from the action of a clear-cut portrayal of a shy, small town boy. Chaplin's character in *The Kid* was rather vague at times—an enigma and an erratic character who spasmodically took action to solve his problems.

In 1924 Buster Keaton's *Sherlock Jr.*, a five-reel feature, exhibited a clever, intricate, smoothly unified story line which made Chaplin's *The Kid* and his three-reel 1923 production, *The Pilgrim*, seem primitive. Story-wise, Chaplin's works in the first part of the Twenties seemed to be fumbling throwbacks to the one- and two-reel comedies of the formative age of the silent screen comedy. Only Chaplin's acting skill and comic ingenuity pulled his works above those of the minor comedians of the times. The key scene in *The Pilgrim* that brought kudos from the critics was the comedian's pantomimed sermon on David and Goliath. A condensed version of my scenario for this three-reel work indicates Chaplin's acting skills:

> Charlie as the bogus minister opens the Bible on the podium, comes forward, and says: "I am going to tell you about David and Goliath . . ." (Title 16). He stretches his hand as high as possible and declares: "Goliath was a very tall man . . ." (Title 17). Charlie now takes a strong man pose and feels his own muscle; he indicates a huge, flowing moustache and flourishes a sword. He moves back and looks into

> the Bible—then back toward the audience, he stoops over and indicates the size of David—about two feet off the floor. He snaps back into the strong man pose and swings a sword. Menacingly he looks down and right. He switches to the David character who is looking up and left. David is pantomimed picking up a stone in a sling and throwing it. The stone is shown by gesticulation as going into the forehead of the giant and plopping out behind. Goliath falls. David is shown cutting off the giant's head and putting it on the end of the sword. The head is then thrown off nonchalantly over the shoulder and given a little Chaplinesque back-kick without looking back. (Chaplin often used this trick with a discarded cigarette.) The little tramp has finished the story; he executes a delicate French-like bow to the left and right and goes off behind the choir box in a run. A little boy claps in the audience. Charlie enters again and bows—runs off left again. He comes back in a flourish and throws kisses to the congregation—opens his arms broadly and clasps his hands together in a victorious salute to himself.

This routine is a brilliant piece of work; Chaplin's sense of timing was never better, his footwork never keener. So, despite weaknesses of the total work, the comedian's genius reigns in such a moment.

The Pilgrim is also interesting because it shows Chaplin using a touch of genteel comedy material. Much of the comedy evolves from the bogus minister's embarrassments when he reverts to his old ways before stuffy, small town people. These people find that their new minister often conducts himself in a worldly way. In the scene described above only a small boy claps at the little tramp's performance; the rest of the congregation are horrified by his theatrics. The parlour scene and eating scene in which he is an invited guest at a Sunday noon meal also rely on the humour of embarrassment. Thus, in this film, his humour more nearly approaches that used by Harold Lloyd in many of the early scenes of *Grandma's Boy*. This was Chaplin's only experiment with this type of material. He could not handle it as effectively as his competitors.

In 1925, however, Chaplin reached a peak with his skilled blend of the serious and the comic in *The Gold Rush*. His virtues finally overbalanced his faults. Some of the golden moments of silent screen comedy were created in this work. Stranded in a small cabin during a blizzard in the Yukon, the little tramp is forced by hunger to eat his own shoe. For this bizarre thanksgiving dinner, Chaplin's skill in comic invention comes into full play. The starved, weary little fellow carves and eats parts of his shoe as if it were turkey. A bent nail from the shoe becomes a wish-bone; and, by an incongruous turn of the little tramp's mind, a side dish on which he has deposited the shoestrings is transformed into a plate of spaghetti. He consequently winds the shoestrings around his fork and devours them with the air of a gourmet. Such comic transposition was Chaplin's forte, and the critics who viewed the film found that such invention would, in the words of *Variety*, "ring the bell."[77] Many evaluators of his work since the first showing of the film have found this scene one of their favourites.

In delicate, facile pantomime *The Gold Rush* has no equal. Furthermore, many of the actions of the little tramp when he was starving have a unique blend of the serious and the comic which were rooted in the character of the lonely little soul. With great pantomimic skill, Chaplin portrays the hollow-eyed, comic hero eyeing the stub of a candle. Sadly the little tramp picks it up and nibbles it with rabbit bites—as if the candle were a piece of carrot or celery. And with a deft touch that shows Chaplin's genius, he sprinkles salt on this morsel of wax, finds that it tastes better, and pops it into his mouth. With such actions a new depth in comic character was added, a dimension that was to make Chaplin the darling of the critics. The comedian was able to make us laugh and still feel sorry for this pathetic little man. The twentieth century, after *The Gold Rush*, seemed to house the reincarnation of the famous nineteenth-century French clown, Jean-Gaspard Debureau, a renowned Pierrot, blended with all the rollicking good spirit of the Clown created by the English music hall's favourite comedian, Grimaldi.

While individual scenes are highly inventive and Chaplin's acting is at a high peak, there are some structural faults in *The Gold Rush*. Although the fewer sequences in the film (nine instead of the fifteen in *The Kid*) seems to tighten the story line, overdrawn exposition develops in the comedy when Chaplin introduces the love interest in sequences that take up twenty minutes running time. The struggles for survival in a remote cabin have already developed lively comedy—nearly three reels of comedy have gone by. A serious, pathetic love attachment then develops when the little tramp sees a beautiful dance hall girl. It takes some effort for Chaplin to return to effective comic episodes, and he needs to get his little tramp back into the wilderness in order to increase the pace and interest in the story.

While Chaplin's use of the motion picture medium generally is very weak, he is able to create excitement in a literal cliff-hanging climactic sequence. The little tramp and his friend

Big Jim McKay are shown caught in a rustic cabin that slips and clings miraculously to the edge of a precipice by a single rope wedged between two rocks and attached to the dwelling. Both Charlie and Big Jim are thrown to the floor of the dwelling that tilts at an angle of over thirty-five degrees. With anguished, perplexed faces, they look up the floor and wonder how they can climb up without the whole cabin slipping into the abyss. The medium takes over: editing, contrasting shots, titles, and special effects help create the comic horror that has been thrust upon the two men. The slipping of the cabin is emphasised by the use of a miniature cabin and cliff—a product of the special effects department in a movie studio.

When Big Jim has hoisted his huge frame on the top of the hapless little tramp, he is able to get out the front door of the cabin. Left alone, poor Charlie doesn't realise that Big Jim has found gold at the edge of the cliff and has forgotten his plight. His cries of help cause the cabin to inch downwards. Finally Big Jim heeds the cries and throws a rope to the little fellow. A process shot shows Charlie coming out of the front door just as the cabin (in miniature) plunges over the edge and into the abyss.

The miniature work, coupled with the process shots, helps greatly to convey the action and develop the comedy. Unfortunately these special effects are rather crude and fall into the same class as the poor exterior scenes of the Yukon territory. There is too much papier-maché and too many poorly painted sets for a film of 1925. Despite this weakness, Chaplin edits the sequence with considerable skill and shows that when he deals with spectacular scenes he can use the medium to assist a comic situation.

While structural defects and use of the medium seemed to be

overlooked, many critics recognised faults in the prolonged resolution of *The Gold Rush.* Theodore Huff felt that the conclusion of the work changed the total "mood" of the film drama by incorporating a happy ending.[11] Robert Payne believed that such an ending was a serious weakness that marred the work because the union of the little tramp and the girl was an improbable resolution.[21] That is, such a union was not consistent with the bent of the characters. I concur with these views. As in *The Kid,* Chaplin has created a lost soul on the fringe of society who is doomed to loneliness. Too much of the ostracised, pathetic Pierrot exists in his comic character to allow a happy ending. Chaplin does not make this mistake in *The Circus.*

Chaplin's last work in the Twenties was created in 1928. While *The Circus* is today one of his least known films, the picture did reveal one of his most poignant moments. A happy ending (which seemed so illogical in *The Kid* and *The Gold Rush*) was avoided. The little tramp is left alone—alone and apart from the circus that has afforded him a taste of fame and excitement. A rival wins the girl he loved, and the child-like little man is shown viewing the long line of circus wagons moving away from him as he leans sadly on his cane in the harsh, early morning sunlight. Chaplin underacts this moment with great skill—suggesting more than he reveals. This glimpse of the sad clown, like other glimpses in the total film, provides a poetic touch which raises Chaplin's works to a meritorious level. A less successful scene, yet highly poignant moment, was created in *The Gold Rush*—but it is more stagey and contrived. Chaplin shows his rejected little fellow looking into a dance hall window, viewing others in the merriment of a New Year's celebration. These two moments in the films provide a key to the understanding of Chaplin's distinguishing characteristic; he was able to create a comedy which effectively blended serious elements with the comic. His rivals were never as successful when they used the same kind of material. Harold Lloyd, for example, tries to promote sympathy for his comic country lad in *Grandma's Boy* and his naive, young social climber in *The Freshman*. But Lloyd overplays the moments in which he might give dimension to his character by this method, and as a result, produces sometimes rather shallow, serious scenes.

Compared with *The Gold Rush*, *The Circus* does not incorporate as much serious material. When the film was reviewed, Robert Sherwood was the only major movie critic who hailed Chaplin's return to stronger, more elaborate comedy scenes. Sherwood felt that his use of rollicking, lively comedy material in his early one- and two-reel works was the essence of the best of Chaplin.[71] There was truth in this view. Many of Chaplin's great acting skills and ingenious gags were created in the gay, nearly irascible, nose-thumbing spirit of his earlier works. His use of the lonely soul is his distinctive feature, but it is only part of the total character. My detailed examination reveals, however, a fault that seemed to be overlooked by Sherwood. While *The Gold Rush* becomes a unified work by showing the tramp's struggle against a hostile environment, no clear, unifying conflict or idea exists in *The Circus*—the story becomes an erratic adventure of a little tramp among circus people. A villainous, exploiting circus manager is a foil for Charlie. This antagonist remains a cliché; he does not have the delightful comic exaggeration of the bullies that inhabit Chaplin's early works. It would seem that Chaplin expects us to take his villain seriously, but we find this pale refugee from the nineteenth-century melodrama (possessing the black hat, black handle-bar moustache, and black heart) a bore after witnessing the antics of the brawny, bear-like villain of *The Gold Rush.*

Making the same error as he did in *The Kid*, Chaplin opens *The Circus* on a serious note that is unimaginative and heavy-handed. When the little tramp is introduced in a lively chase sequence with a pickpocket, the comic story line begins to sparkle.

It should be noted that in this neglected work there are many laughable scenes that are worthy of Chaplin. His comic pantomime is nimble and suave. While it may be classified as an uneven work with many faults, it is by far a greater work than the much applauded first feature, *The Kid*. Even though the nine sequences of this work are not ostensibly tied together with a strong, clear-cut comic idea, it is still an adventure that holds the attention of an audience viewing the work today.

In *The Circus* Chaplin also creates many clever comic scenes which surpass those of his earlier works. The little tramp's feeble attempts to be a clown in a circus produce ingenious comedy which reveals an inept little fellow who is most funny when he makes mistakes in executing his clown routines. Combining great danger with his comedy in a fashion which probably reflected the influence of Harold Lloyd's *Safety Last*, Chaplin shows his comic character trying to escape from the cage of a sleeping lion in which he has been accidentally trapped; and the little fellow executes comical, involuntary arabesques on a high wire when he is forced into substituting for the star performer. Such situations encompass some of the most laughable moments in Chaplin's works.

With the coming of sound in the final years of the Twenties, Chaplin's *The Circus* concluded his efforts in silent screen drama. Even though *City Lights* in 1931 used no human speech, music and sound effects on the soundtrack were evidence that the comedian was being dragged stubbornly into the world of sound from the marvellous world of silence. It was in this land of black and white—shadows and light—that Chaplin created some of his best work. Each of the features being examined in this study shows the treatment of its story material using sweeping, sentimental strokes. Unlike the other comedians of the Twenties, Chaplin was a sentimentalist and a romantic. Comedians Lloyd, Keaton and Langdon experimented with comic versions of the struggles of a little man—a little man who seemed to be a comic counterpart of the Horatio Alger, Jr. hero —a simple, honest young man who becomes a success. Chaplin avoided this material, generally, even though his peremptory happy endings seemed to be influenced by such subject matter. *The Kid*, with slight updating, seemed like a variation on a Charles Dickens novel; *The Circus* had material akin to the struggles of Pierrot, with the juxtapositioning of Harlequin-like slapstick; and *The Gold Rush*, seemingly less distant and very specific, still had material treated with broad strokes and abstracted from reality through Chaplin's romanticism.

Several major conclusions may be drawn from all this. Chaplin's works are marked by strong assets and deficits. One of his greatest faults lies in his awkward story telling. His greatest virtues, his acting skill and his comic invention, however, made him the master of silent screen pantomime.

Analysis also leads me to the conclusion that *The Gold Rush*, with all its faults, is superior to the other two features that have been discussed. It achieves a higher degree of unity by using the strong central idea of the frail tramp struggling against great odds on the Alaskan frontier. A reversal of roles and a burlesque treatment of the adventures of the wild northland seem to operate to achieve the comic in this work. Among rugged "he-men" of the Yukon, the little tramp cuts a laughable figure as he weakly faces storms, men crazy for gold, and starvation.

The failure to unify his works, however, is evident in his other films of the Twenties—not only his features but his one- to three-reel works. A close investigation of his works will expose this weakness. I find the works of Harold Lloyd, Buster Keaton, and Harry Langdon much better than Chaplin's in this respect; they were much better story-tellers. Lloyd achieved unity through strong central comic ideas in three of his famous works: *Grandma's Boy* (1922), *Safety Last* (1923), and *The Freshman* (1926). Keaton's *Sherlock Jr.* (1924), and Langdon's *Long Pants* (1927) were unified in the same way and exhibited a tightness of solid continuity lacking in Chaplin's films.

While this study concentrates on the comic films of the Twenties, the era which has been called the golden age of comedy, it cannot overlook Chaplin's later works. He attempted to continue the silent screen tradition into the formative period of the sound film. At least one more masterpiece, *City Lights*, came from the famous comedian's effort to continue his work in the older mode. Essentially this 1931 film was a silent picture created in the infant years of the "talkies". Chaplin was warned of the financial risk—that people wanted films with spoken dialogue. Nevertheless, he used merely a musical score and limited sound effects for the soundtrack of the film. This was, therefore, a silent movie.

Despite the lack of human voice, few people objected; *City Lights* made a profit of five million dollars. And rightly so; it was a critical success. In many ways this film is the equal of *The Gold Rush.* With fewer weaknesses in story line than Chaplin's 1928 *The Circus*, it achieved unity by using a central comic idea in the manner of *The Gold Rush.*

While *City Lights* has the initial look of a contemporary film on a contemporary subject, it definitely is not. The romantic-sentimental spirit of Chaplin's main body of work is revealed. The big city seems like a far-off place—somewhere in Europe, possibly. The home of the blind girl, acted by Virginia Cherrill, has the look of a poor Spanish courtyard and is reached by an archway from the city streets. In short, the environment is a synthesis that suited Chaplin's romantic view. The work is subtitled "A Comedy Romance in Pantomine." There is a unique juxtapositioning of pathos and knockabout farce in the film that has made it a favourite of many critics. But there is a clumsiness in the structure of the work that is disconcerting; the pace of the work sometimes becomes too slow as transitional scenes focusing on the blind girl's plight are used between fast-moving comedy scenes.

Some of Chaplin's innovations in comedy are revealed when the little tramp is befriended by a drunk millionaire. At a night club the inebriated Charlie mistakes an apache dance for the real thing and tries to save the girl from what he believes is a dreadful mauling by a Parisian rowdy. As he eats spaghetti, the celebrating crowd throws confetti and a streamer of the paper lands in his plate; unaware, drunkenly intent on his eating, he chews away on the paper as if it were a very long piece of spaghetti—rising from his chair, stretching and nibbling as if he were headed toward the ceiling.

By far the funniest scene occurs when Charlie takes the desperate step to provide money for the blind girl. Chaplin revives and refurbishes material from his 1914 *The Knockout*, and his 1915 *The Champion*. Forced into a quick money scheme, he finds himself fighting in the ring with a person of superior ability. Realising his inferiority, Charlie does not play the game; he avoids the prize-fighter by his dance-like, ring-around-the-rosy effort, keeping the referee between the brutal pugilist and himself. The whole sequence is lively, colourful and extremely funny.

A sequence preceding this portion of the film shows some of the older, cruder forms of humour being employed. Charlie tries to make friends with his opponent in the locker room. His overtures are delicate and effete. He smiles and twists his head coyly, grasping his own knees with his hands in a childlike gesture of friendship. The tough, ape-like boxers around him are appalled. His opponent retreats into a curtained room to change into his boxing trunks. Homosexuality as material for humour, therefore, was used in an age when it was a taboo. But Chaplin's skill was great, and he was able to execute the gag with the finesse to make it acceptable.

And finally, the "pathos" which Chaplin employed reached its greatest height. Theodore Huff aptly describes the quality of the last scene:

> The equivocal ending of the film, ironic and vibrant with the tragic sense of life, seldom fails to bring tears. The terrified smile of the tramp at the girl who has recovered her vision through him, and through that recovery is lost to him, is one of the most poignant scenes ever photographed.[11]

At this moment the dialogue used in the titles is effectively simple, and the power of understatement contrasts with the visual:

"You can see now?"

"Yes, I can see now."

And this is the end. The little tramp's smile is strangely

twisted; his fingers and the rose she has given him touch the edge of the Pierrot mask.

Chaplin's next film, *Modern Times* (1936), was the comedian's last attempt to retain the silent film tradition. A few concessions were made to the sound film; he allowed the sound of the human voice over a television set (a factory's closed-circuit TV system was employed comically—as in George Orwell's 1984 "Big Brother is watching you" television device). And Chaplin permitted the human voice for a radio and a record player. Finally, his most interesting concession: for one routine in the last portion of the film, Chaplin sang.

This work sums up all the comedian's virtues and faults. One of the last bursts of Chaplin's great comic invention and acting skill, *Modern Times* is an anthology with many of the comedian's old gags refurbished. We see him battling with cops and stuffed-shirts as he did in his Essanay and Mutual two-reelers; he confronts both bullies and gentle people, as in his feature works of the Twenties. He shows he can fight with amazing footwork, roller-skate with comic dignity, and juggle a tray laden with a mountain of food as he encounters drunks and dancers. And the man-child is also capable of falling in love. While many critics see the comedian engaging in strong satire, they fail to note the emphasis on warmth and gaiety in his fun-making. Chaplin is at his best when he burlesques the factory worker turned into a trained ape; or when he gathers his shabby dignity and confronts authority with the best air a little man can muster. Also we see the very human tenderness of the tramp who looks for a kind gesture in a cold, self-centred world. Episodic and meandering in its story line, *Modern Times* had dramatic weaknesses that tainted the total work, but the human figure of the little tramp never glowed brighter.

The last fully drawn portrait of the Little Tramp appears in MODERN TIMES (1936). Symbolically, he walks towards the hills never to return.

LIMELIGHT (1953) shows the last important effort of Chaplin as he creates the portrait of a fading music hall comedian.

Right: Mabel Normand in the genteel comedy MICKEY (1916-8) which revealed Sennett's attempt to develop features with material often associated with a Mary Pickford film.
Below: Wallace Reid (left) starred in THE DANCIN' FOOL (1920), a light comedy that was typical of the times. In it, a country boy moves to the city and becomes a success.

While critics have overlooked some of Chaplin's faults, their praise of his acting skill and his comic invention is generally sound. Chaplin was a master at both broad, acrobatic pantomime and simple routines that demanded slight hand movements and facial expressions. He was able to make smoking a cigarette and counting money extremely funny—slight things to be sure, but he firmly based his comedy on the eccentricities of the little tramp. His comic invention sprang from the unusual way this clown faced the world—whether it was battling a bully or spreading butter on his pancakes. Furthermore, Chaplin had an acting intensity that was unique. He seemed to believe in his little tramp and to become so much a part of the strange world he created for the character that almost everyone believed (and still does) that it could hardly be an actor playing the role. In fact, he became so identified with the role that many of his fans and the critics were disappointed with his sophisticated comic character, Henri Verdoux, in the 1947 film, *Monsieur Verdoux.*

The world of silence was Chaplin's medium. There are many moments in *The Great Dictator* (1940), *Monsieur Verdoux*, and *Limelight* (1953) that are worthy of Chaplin's genius. To me, however, his last great work is *Modern Times* in 1936. His tramp remains in the world of silence—except for a song in the latter portion of the film. A new dimension is added to the little fellow—one hitherto unseen. The little tramp, the entertainer, is revealed. He dances and breaks into a gay, charming song:

El pwu el se domtroco
La spinach or la tuko
Cigaretto toto torlo
E rusho spagaletto

4

Senora ce la tima
Voulez vous la taxi meter
Le jonta tu la zita
Je le tu le tu le twaa

La der la ser pawnbroker
Lusern apprer how mucher
E se confess a potcha
Ponka walla ponka wa.*

It was a swan song; only a faint image of the tramp-clown existed in Chaplin's films from then on. The little tramp, urging his girl to smile and face a new dawn, walked down the road at the end of the film for the last time.

3. Comedy Dons a New Suit

AS THE ODD, moustached little tramp who existed on the fringes of society waddled over the hills, he was replaced by the young man next door who came striding over the horizon with a naive determination to take the world by the tail. The polite or genteel comedy, in fact, seemed to threaten the life of forthright, ebullient slapstick. The movement only changed the focus and moderated the older tradition, but its influence was felt by the four great clowns of the silent screen.

*First words spoken by Chaplin for the film as recorded in a review of *Modern Times.*[74] The comedian's pantomime and vocal inflection help make sense of this manufactured language—a whimsy of Chaplin's creation.

> Burlesque and farce are becoming less and less popular, and there is no real demand for stories of this type. The comedy producers are desirous of polite, plausible situation comedies, preferably founded upon an amusing situation that might very naturally occur in the life of almost any spectator.[51]

Frederick Palmer expressed this view in 1922 as he criticised a two-reel Christie comedy called *Her Bridal Nightmare* in a book which was intended to be a guide for scenario writers. If this statement is viewed with the historical perspective of today, it is obvious that Palmer overstated the situation. Many slapstick-filled burlesques and farces were ground out by the Mack Sennett and Hal Roach comedy mills even in the late Twenties. There was a trend, however, which formed the basis for this overstatement.

Genteel comedy's invasion of the screen world was helped greatly by the success of the short films of John Bunny and the comedy team of Mr. and Mrs. Sidney Drew. As this type of drama took a firm grip in the 1910's, a wealth of light comedy actresses came into the limelight. Such famous women as Mary Pickford, Dorothy Gish, Zasu Pitts, and Mabel Normand found light comedy features their province. Mary Pickford had preceded Bunny and the Drews in her exploitation of polite comedy filled with sentiment. In fact so much emphasis was placed on sentiment that the term comedy would hardly seem to apply to her films. Dorothy Gish, a name not usually associated with comedy, scored a success in D. W. Griffith's *Hearts of the World* (1918) and went on to make such films as *Battling Jane*, a domestic comedy with a war background. Zasu Pitts, who was to do an excellent serious portrait of Trina in von Stroheim's classic *Greed* (1923), was featured in many light comedies during the same period. But by far the most interesting comedienne to embrace the genteel tradition was Mabel Normand.

Miss Normand was schooled by Mack Sennett in the rough and tumble world of slapstick. She was known as a deft thrower (and receiver) of the custard pie. In August, 1916, Sennett had Bob Jones, a heretofore slapstick director and stunt man, launch into a full length film that was spiritually far removed from the wild capers of *Tillie's Punctured Romance*. It was a sentimental rags-to-riches movie that would have fitted Mary Pickford perfectly. A brief synopsis of the film's story from a contemporary review reveals the well worn Cinderella story from the popular magazine fiction of the age:

> Mickey has been brought up with little regard for conventions out West. Her aunt, believing she owns a gold mine, invites her East, but upon finding she has no money, puts her to work as a servant. While West, Mickey has met and fallen in love with a wealthy young man her aunt had intended to marry her daughter to, but he had, instead been captured by Mickey, so when he, too, comes East, he manages to free himself from aunty's designs and marries Mickey instead.[55]

As Eileen Bowser, Assistant Curator of the Museum of Modern Art Film Library, so aptly observes, the film employs material like that used by Mary Pickford: "In *The Foundling*, made the year before *Mickey*, Miss Pickford had played a similar and typical part, that of the mischievous and innocent little orphan, loved by all right-thinking people and abused by the evil ones."*

*From Eileen Bowser's unpublished programme notes on *Stenographer Wanted* (1912), *Goodness Gracious* (1914) and *Mickey* (1916–1918).

What, one may ask, is funny about such material? The answer may be a simple: "Not much." The basic material for the polite or genteel comedy is often lacking in a strong central comic idea. Comedy seems grafted onto a serious plot. After viewing such works I believe that the actor or director has often injected comic routines or simple comic business during the shooting of the scenes, but some humorous elements are obviously written into the script. In *Mickey*, for example, some comic traits of a mild, humorous nature can be observed in the tomboyish activities of the title character. When the heroine is going to be spanked for her misbehaviour, she feeds the instrument for punishment, a razor strap, to a donkey. Also, in high society, Mickey's bad manners are a subject for comedy. The film nearly engages in slapstick, but restrains itself, when Mickey's Western "parents", Joe and his fat Indian housekeeper, get into altercations with high society. In a final melodramatic fight between the hero and the villain, a burlesque treatment in the one- and two-reel Sennett tradition would seem a likely direction for the film. But director Bob Jones seems to have held back his natural inclinations. He designs the sequence to be taken seriously.

With all its faults, curiously enough, the film has a flair. By modern standards, it cannot be considered a comedy of great merit. Mabel Normand's skill as an actress, her spark and charm, however, save *Mickey*.

Women were not, of course, the most important promoters of the genteel comedy. Light comedians like Douglas MacLean, Charles Ray, Wallace Reid, and Johnny Hines advanced this type of film both in theory and practice. Each of these comedians dealt with material that Harold Lloyd was to employ with considerably more skill.

Johnny Hines, for example, created a two-reel Torchy series in the late 1910's in which light comedy situations revolved around the trials of the "average American boy next door."[19] In the Twenties, Hines acted in many feature length works with such titles as *Burn 'Em Up Barnes*, *Luck*, *The Early Bird*, and *Live Wire*—comedies which, as the titles indicate, displayed the comedy of a young man trying to make good. Bernard Sobel's review of Hines's *Burn 'Em Up Barnes* reveals the nature of the material used in this film. Evidently the film used slick magazine story material involving a devil-may-care protagonist who was addicted to speeding around town in a racing car.[72] An advertisement in *The Film Year Book 1925* makes capital of this quality by pointing out the virtues of Johnny Hines's comic character. Hines "typifies the American Go-getter", the advertisement reads as it announces that Hines's films offer "clean, smart, wholesome comedy that will be an inspiration to the youth of the land."[46]

Douglas MacLean, another popular comedian during the late 1910's and early Twenties, seemed to have employed a character similar to Hines's. Again, turning to the reviews of Bernard Sobel in the *Dramatic Mirror*, the reader can see MacLean following the pattern of the magazine short story. In *One a Minute*, MacLean created a young promoter who is efficient and hard working; he discovers a panacea drug that cures everyone and makes him financially successful.[73] John Montgomery classifies MacLean's output as "polite farces."[19]

In 1919 comedian Charles Ray appeared in a feature-length film, *The Sheriff's Son*, a work which displays many similarities to Lloyd's *Grandma's Boy* (1922). In theme, the two works are strikingly similar. In *The Sheriff's Son*, Ray plays the role of a meek, cowardly boy who overcomes a gang of outlaws despite his reputation for cowardliness.[54] A year later Ray appeared in a feature-length comedy called *Homer Comes Home*, a work which related a tale of a young man going to the big city to gain employment as a clerk; he becomes successful enough to be given a managerial post in his home town, and he wins the girl friend who has waited for him back home. Homer, the reviewer points out, was "another addition to Charles Ray's long string of country lads who make good in spite of tremendous odds."[52]

Although Wallace Reid was not considered a high-ranking comedian in the late 1910's and the early Twenties, he was a popular star who was versatile enough to play in both serious and comic works. In 1920 he applied his talents to a comic film with all the ingredients of the Hines, Ray, and MacLean features. From the popular literature of the time, Reid's enactment of a rural comic type, called Sylvester Tibble, provided another portrait of a young man striving for success. In this film, *The Dancin' Fool*, the young man from the country looks for his fortune in the big city. With the ambition characteristic of the Horatio Alger hero,* he sets his uncle's business on a profitable basis by putting his ingenuity to work over his uncle's resistance to a country lad who, the uncle feels, is not a responsible addition to his factory.

Like *Mickey*, *The Dancin' Fool* incorporates sympathetic roles that an audience feels are close to their own lives. At least, it provides the illusion of characters that are known or might be encountered even though personal identification is not present. Such characters are warm and gentle; they have

*Horatio Alger, Jr., an American writer of popular fiction in the late 19th century, is considered the person most responsible for promoting the "rags-to-riches" theme in popular literature. This theme was often used in the magazine short story and the light comedy film of the Twenties.

ambitions and tastes similar to those of the average man. They are not the odd, outcast protagonists of the slapstick tradition.

Three of the major comedians of the Twenties, Lloyd, Keaton, and Langdon, were influenced by the genteel tradition but were generally able to avoid its fault by retaining the spirit of and much material from the slapstick tradition. Lloyd, more than the other two, drew heavily on both the story material and the characterisations of the genteel comedy. When he created the young, shy character whose most distinguishing feature was large, horn-rimmed glasses, he wrote:

> A picture actor named Mortenson, who lived in the same apartment house on Fourth Street just off the Hill, and I talked over its [the comic character's] possibilities night after night. The glasses would serve as my trademark and at the same time suggest the character—quiet, normal, boyish, clean, sympathetic, not impossible to romance. I would need no eccentric make-up, "mo" or funny clothes. I would be an average recognizable American youth and let the situation take care of the comedy. The comedy should be better for not depending upon a putty nose or its equivalent and the situations would be better for not being tied to low-comedy coat tails; funnier things happen in life to an ordinary boy than to a Lonesome Luke. Exaggeration is the breath of picture comedies, and obviously they cannot be true to life, but they can be recognizably related to life.[17]

But Lloyd did not create a sentimental portrait. He blended many facets which the polite comedians used and many that were different. In the shy young man there was a degree of will or determination that took on some of the characteristics which

Douglas MacLean and Johnny Hines employed in their comic portraits. Furthermore, and probably most important of all, he did not reject as many of the facets of the slapstick character as the above quotation would seem to indicate. He retained an aggressiveness in his comic character that was similar to the comedian's bold spirit when he faced opposition in his early one- and two-reel comedies. In moments of desperation in the feature-length works of the 1920's, Lloyd's character took drastic steps—he even stole a car or struck a policeman to achieve his goal.

Lloyd, therefore, was eclectic in the development of his comic character. The added dimension and flexibility of comic portrayal which resulted from such a practice may account in part for his eclipsing of the "country boys" and "go-getters" in popularity.

To a lesser degree, Keaton and Langdon changed their comic characters under the influence of the genteel comedy. When Keaton turned to features, his portrayal was altered to provide a broader basis for comic variety and story development. His John McKay of *Our Hospitality* (1923) takes on the facets of a determined young man who desires to claim his inheritance and win the affections of a girl. In his one- and two-reel works, Keaton's character was usually that of a little outcast without connections—without a family or a place to go. His *Sherlock, Jr.* (1924) and *The General* (1927) feature comic protagonists who are small town boys with some of the same traits and problems of the genteel comedy character. Langdon retained modified traits of the little tramp in his *Strong Man* (1926) and turned toward the country lad in his *Long Pants* (1927). However, his modulation of character under the influence of genteel comedy was not as strong as either Lloyd's or Keaton's.

All three comedians dipped heavily into the plot materials of the genteel comedy. Lloyd's works, *Grandma's Boy* (1922), *Safety Last* (1923), and *The Freshman* (1925) are comic variations on the success story. Personal, business, and social achievement are essayed in a laughable way. Keaton's comic character was driven by child-like desire to be a detective in *Sherlock, Jr.* and a soldier in *The General*. Such desires were the mainspring of the plot development in his films. Less endowed with will than the comic portraits of Lloyd and Keaton, Langdon's character wistfully desired to be a man and a great lover in *Long Pants*.

While these three comedians used some of the same type of story material employed by Charles Ray, Douglas MacLean, and Johnny Hines, they handled their material differently. They did not directly adapt material from the literature of the day, nor did they employ a scenario as did these light comedians. Their working method remained more flexible by the retention of the off-the-cuff story plotting and shooting methods of the one- and two-reel comedies of the 1910's. On the other hand, Ray, MacLean, and Hines were often bound to the incidents of the magazine short story or the comic stage play. Such works as Hines's *The Live Wire*, MacLean's *One a Minute*, and Ray's *The Sheriff's Son* and *Homer Comes Home* are adaptations.

This more flexible method of handling story materials allowed Lloyd, Keaton, and Langdon greater latitude in developing their comedies. The story could be patterned to their acting abilities and to the characters they were portraying. Gags could arise from improvisation while shooting a scene. It would seem that such a working method would lead to episodic story development, but the comedians were usually able to prevent this by their strong control on production details and by constantly reminding themselves and their writers of the total flow of the dramatic story. Keaton effectively explained the way in which the top comedians of the Twenties held their creations firmly in their own hands:

> We worked hard. We stayed with the story all of the way. In the old days all of us—Chaplin, Lloyd, Harry Langdon, and myself—worked with our writers from the day they started the story. We checked on the scenery, the cast, the locations—often going on trips with the unit managers to pick these out ourselves and make sure they were suitable. We directed our own pictures, working up our own gags as we went along, saw rushes, supervised the cutting, went to the sneak previews. . . . We were the ones who decided what should go into a script to make an audience laugh.[14]

But Chaplin held firmly to his little tramp. Some argument might be advanced to support the view that his 1921 production of *The Kid* came under the influence of genteel comedy. There is enough sentimental material in the work to make it qualify, but Chaplin casts this work into a different spirit. An incurable romantic, he remains individualistic in his treatment. There is something of the past—something out of Dickens—in Chaplin that seems to refurbish anything which might smack of genteel comedy by recasting it into the spirit of an older tradition. His 1925 version of the Yukon, *The Gold Rush*, is a romance, almost an epic comedy, that was several mountain ranges removed from the valley inhabited by the country lads and the go-getters.

4. A Young Man Going Up

HIS TEETH caught sunbeams under his horn-rimmed glasses, and his straw hat sometimes tilted back in a careless manner or, on other occasions, sat at the proper angle of a young man who might succeed. Shy and respectful with girls, he sometimes assumed a frantic, leonine nature as he dashed to the rescue with his coat tails flying. His ready smile was eclipsed by agonised lips when a bold scheme backfired. But he was not a pouting Pierrot—he was Harlequin the Happy of the silent screen. Forever moving, generally in an upward direction, he was cloaked in a gaiety and charm all his own. By pluck or luck he was a match for any Punch or Scaramouche that might be his rival, and he finally would get Columbine for his own.

But Harold Lloyd's first comic film in 1915 received this short, scathing review:

> JUST NUTS (Pathé)—An exaggerated slapstick comedy that the title fully describes. It is neither funny nor original and has little about it in any way. The incidents are exceedingly disconnected, and are not in themselves funny.[65]

While Lloyd claims he avoided copying the character of Chaplin, *Just Nuts* is a very Chaplinesque work. Lloyd used a tramp-clown character attired in big shoes and pants, with a sharp eye on the women in the park. This outcast obnoxiously took what he wanted. He grabbed a cigar from a portly man's mouth, took a paper (and spectacles to read it) from a sleeping man on a park bench. As the review aptly stated, *Just Nuts* was a disjointed work. But it was a beginning—an experiment.

The Willie Work one-reel films which followed and the Lonesome Luke series showed a degree of improvement over this first major venture into the comic film. The new comedy character, Lonesome Luke, was instituted the same year that the primitive *Just Nuts* was produced. According to a review, better material improved Lloyd's work slightly:

> LONESOME LUKE (Pathe)—written by "Tad," the well-known cartoonist, this split-reel comedy, though entirely lacking in originality and utilizing time-worn features still has several amusing parts. A bear escapes from a menagerie and a prisoner in jail is offered his freedom to don a bear skin and enter a cage with a lion. He enters the cage, but immediately becomes afraid, and escaping into the audience causes consternation, until he is finally captured by an alleged comedy police department.[66]

This brief synopsis and evaluation of the film reveal a fantastic situation in the Mack Sennett tradition, a tradition of comedy which incorporated the violent and the absurd. The use of a "comedy police department" also indicates an imitation of the famous Keystone Cops.

Harold Lloyd, it should be noted, was employed by a producing group that imitated, as did other producing companies, the successful split-reel,* one-reel and two-reel comedies of the day. The use of the comic chase became a stock situation for many films. John B. Kennedy quotes Lloyd's evaluation of this

*Many short comedies, like the above-mentioned *Lonesome Luke*, were not a full reel in length. The producer often filled out the reel with brief travelogue or "nature study" material. The term applied to this incongruous combination was "spit-reel comedy."

practice: "Our record week's output was three. Wide, heavy slapstick on the simplest theme—eight hundred feet of so-called plot. Whatever the plot, the picture always ended with two hundred feet of chase."[37] With this emphasis on stock situation and slapstick, the comic character portrayed was obviously very sketchily drawn in his early films.

Following the prolific production procedures of his contemporaries and predecessors, Lloyd, under the direction of Hal Roach, turned out numerous Lonesome Luke films from 1915 through 1917. The U.S. Copyright publication, *Motion Pictures*: 1912-1939, lists such titles as *Lonesome Luke in Stop! Luke! Listen!*, *Lonesome Luke from London to Laramie*, *Lonesome Luke—Mechanic*, *Lonesome Luke—Plumber*, and many more. Harold Lloyd's output in his formative years as a comedian was so great that he tired of comic clothes and the character of Lonesome Luke "after more than sixty" films.[38]

But Lloyd's comic acting skills were developing rapidly in his apprenticeship with the Lonesome Luke character. In *Lonesome Luke—Movie Operator*, Lloyd demonstrated some touches of the gaiety and charm that were to be his trademark. As a movie theatre manager, he smiled broadly and innocently at a beautiful woman. Such flirting, of course, promoted a punch in the nose from the husband. And, much like the gay fellow of his later films, Luke shed this misfortune and ushered more patrons to their seats in the movie theatre.

By 1917, the year that Charles Chaplin was producing some of his best two-reel works for Mutual Films, the Lonesome Luke series featured two-reel films. Evidence of the comedian's growth was revealed in a review of *Lonesome Luke's Wild Women.*[53] While the reviewer notes the use of "rough slapstick" in this film, he also comments on the cleverness and originality in the pantomime which Lloyd incorporated into this two-reel work. He prophetically adds that Lloyd's use of "farce-comedy" might prove successful in a five-reel, feature-length work.*

But Harold Lloyd continued with one- and two-reel works even after he had abandoned the Lonesome Luke character. In a slow evolutionary process, his works revealed a tendency to develop a more realistic comic character when he donned his trademark, the horn-rimmed glasses, in 1917. In 1918 he turned out many one-reel comedies with such titles as *Take a Chance*, *Look Out Below*, *Bride and Gloom*, and *On the Jump*. A 1918 one-reel work, *Back Stage*, reveals a curious hybrid in the comedian's comic character. As a happy-go-lucky stage hand, Lloyd's character wears a derby, baggy pants, and large comedy shoes; but the character also wears the now-famous horn-rimmed glasses. He has some of the same over-eagerness and naivete of his later characterisations. A loosely constructed work, *Back Stage* is, in many ways, a throwback to earlier comedies. There are many broad slapstick routines. Some of the routines, however, are cleverly executed by Lloyd in a style that is similar to Charles Chaplin's 1917 work in two-reel films. At one point in the film the comedian appears to run down a stair-well. He comes "up" again and folds the "stair-well" into what is really a stage flat. The stage hand also assumes the role of a Hindu snake charmer to get a snake out of the room in the theatre. Such routines are reminiscent of the English music hall theatre; an examination of Charles Chaplin's 1917 output

*Critics and reviewers of this time assigned a genre classification of "farce-comedy" to a work that exhibited strong plot and character development. The use of improbable situations in comedy was being frowned on by the critics.

reveals similar pantomime incidents. This minor work, more than any film Lloyd produced, thus shows a remote link with the *commedia dell' arte* tradition. Tangential routines in *Back Stage* have the characteristics of a *lazzi* of this ancient theatrical mode—for such "comic bits" are short pantomime incidents that display the skills of the leading comedian.

The year after *Back Stage* was created, 1919, *Just Neighbors* was produced. This work clearly reveals a transition to a new comic character taking place. Lloyd's comic character is shown in a quiet suburban setting; he is a young, eager, white-collar worker wearing a neat suit, a straw hat, and a disarming, infectious smile. Interestingly enough, his neighbour, played by Harry "Snub" Pollard, still wears the habit of the traditional clown and has a large walrus moustache. Only when an altercation with his neighbour leads to a comic fist fight does Lloyd return to the gross slapstick like that employed in the earlier work, *Back Stage*.

The slapstick, farcical situations which still permeated Lloyd's work in 1918 and 1919 reveal the comedian's link with his predecessors. The transition from the old to the new tradition from 1917 to 1922 was not so clear-cut as Lloyd's reminiscences would seem to indicate in his 1928 autobiography. The older tradition was still apparent in his works. In the early portion of *High and Dizzy* (1920), the comic character which Lloyd had established in 1917 is strong; it is a portrait of a youthful, over-eager doctor who falls in love with a beautiful girl who enters his office. When this character gets drunk, however, a large portion of the film returns to a more genteel version of the older slapstick comedies. As a drunk, the young man becomes brazen and mischievous. He engages in many altercations with people on the street and in a hotel. When he sobers up again and meets

Faulty clothes create comedy in Harold Lloyd's first feature, GRANDMA'S BOY (1922).

The use of the camera and editing for comedy: what appears to be the death house in one shot of SAFETY LAST (1923) turns out to be a railway station in the next. Comedian Lloyd is in the centre.

The thrill comedy of Harold Lloyd: five shots from the famous scene in SAFETY LAST (1923 and (bottom right) one shot from FEET FIRST (1930) in which Lloyd tried to recapture the success of the earlier film with a similar episode.

the young girl, he reverts to the pleasant young man. Only to a degree does Lloyd use the light, realistic comedy with sentimental overtones.

This work and its precursor, *Look Out Below* (1918), also illustrate Lloyd's exploitation of what he called the "thrill picture"—a film comedy that depended for its laughs on dangerous incidents atop a high building. The success of this type of material led him to produce many variations on this kind of film: *Never Weaken* (1921), another two-reeler; and the popular features, *Safety Last* (1923), *Welcome Danger* (1929), and *Feet First* (1930).

Get Out and Get Under, a two-reel work that was created a few months after *High and Dizzy*, shows Lloyd's character evolving into its final form. As an owner of a new car Harold beams with pride. He is an optimistic soul with a wide smile for all who see him driving his car. The smile becomes increasingly hard to maintain as he meets many obstacles with his automobile. The character is shown in a lively, colourful gamut of frustration.

Harold Lloyd needed only one more year of two-reel films to set his skills firmly for a broader canvas. While Keaton's and Chaplin's switch to feature-length work was clearly by design, Lloyd's move toward the full-length film was evolutionary and unannounced. He expanded his material as he obtained a firmer grasp on character and plot in his many one- and two-reel works. According to Lloyd, both *A Sailor Made Man* in 1921 and *Grandma's Boy* in 1922, his first four- and five-reel comedies, were produced under a two-reel contract.[17] *A Sailor Made Man*, Lloyd's last "short work," indicated that he had handled his material with greater skill than in previous pictures. When he wrote in retrospect about his creation of this four-reel film, the comedian realised the merit of a strong central idea to unify the story line:

> I played a rich young fellow who thought he could have and could do anything he wanted. Through a sequence of incidents he enlists in the navy and, much against his will, goes to sea. They take all the nonsense out of him there. His shipmates make a man of him, before they get through. So you see that the central idea was a real one; that hard knocks will bring out a man's mettle, if he has any.[40]

Lloyd's work was also better because of the pains that he took to build up each comic incident. A comic fight in which his character, without engaging in combat himself, cleverly got his best friend to fight eight men, was elaborately planned and executed.[40] Lloyd became, therefore, a creator who was aware of the fine points of comedy and story development. At the turning point of his career, it is little wonder that he later revealed his satisfaction with *A Sailor Made Man*: "I felt that I had at last arrived somewhere."[40]

Indeed, Lloyd had placed himself beside Chaplin. His first feature, *Grandma's Boy*, was before the public's eyes only a year after Chaplin released *The Kid*. In his film, Lloyd followed a different path from Chaplin's by combining slapstick with genteel humour. He employed some of the same plot complications used by Charles Ray, Wallace Reid, and Douglas MacLean, but he blended sequences of slapstick into the work. With this combination he exerted all his skill; his comic invention, his snappy paced stories, and his gay, energetic comic character produced outstanding features in the Twenties. Lloyd quickly rose from the ranks of minor comedians and became a popular and critical success.

Chaplin was a worker of considerable vitality and tenacity. His output in the 1910's was not as fruitful in number of comedies, but in his Mutual period (1916–1917) he created twelve two-reel comedies in eighteen months. Lloyd and Keaton outstripped him in the long run—at least in number of works. Lloyd, during his early one- and two-reel period, was the most prolific of all the major comedians. Nelson E. Garringer tried to list his early works in *Films in Review*,[57] and even though some of these films are not on the copyright records, Garringer was able to set down the titles of over 125 one- and two-reel comedies. This does not include Lloyd's one-reel works in 1915 and 1916—the age when Hal Roach was careless in getting his films copyrighted. Therefore, it could be concluded that Lloyd made nearly two hundred short films or about thirty one- and two-reel works a year before he created features.

While this prolific output certainly provided the comedian with the experience necessary to make better feature works—that is, he handled a wide range of comic material and attempted to get new twists in content—the routine of grinding out a work frequently produced negative results. Certainly, many of his early films had the rough cleverness and vitality of a Sennett work, but they were often as thin in quality. Unlike Chaplin, Lloyd did not free himself from the dangers of the comedy mill as early as he should have.

Evidently there was a trait of co-operativeness in Lloyd that was a virtue and a fault. He accepted the system more easily than Chaplin—a fault that Keaton also possessed. But Lloyd worked well with the established system without dire consequences. He controlled more than he was led—his ability to stand forth as an individual, as the leading creator of his films, and as a charming screen personality did not break down until his last sound pictures. In the Twenties he had a strength of will and a determination that enabled him to do his best work. Generally he fulfilled the role of master comedian, and his film reflected his desire for perfection.

In a June, 1965 interview, he told me how he acquired some of the enterprising traits of his comedy character. As a boy he sold popcorn to passengers on the trains that stopped in Omaha, Nebraska.* He confessed that he drew upon some of his own personality—a go-getting trait that he had, but emphasised the fact that he had to abstract from life. He placed the facets of the eager and bungling young man into comic perspective; he meant to parody or genially poke fun at the American dream of success.

In the films of Lloyd and Keaton there is a strong sense of cause and effect even when the situation borders on the fantastic. They had a love of the logical and the mechanical. Lloyd had a concern for gadgets. Throughout his pictures his protagonist became entangled with automobiles, streetcars and bicycles. Objects of all kinds promoted the comic frustration of his character. Also, his eager young man used machines in an odd way—much like Keaton used his locomotives, steamships, and motorcycles—and drove them unlike anyone else. As a boy Lloyd was keen on hobbies and is still a collector in his retirement.

A love of life and a curiosity about many things (traits possessed by Chaplin) developed Lloyd's versatility. He was capable of handling a variety of material because of his many interests. He maintained a gamut of story ideas even in his

*Details of his business are given in the autobiography *An American Comedy*. Lloyd tells of his success in this venture—how he netted from twelve to fifteen dollars a week, a good deal of money for a boy at that time.

features. When he repeated some basic idea, such as the "thrill-comedy" showing his protagonist caught up in a difficult climb up the side of a building, his concern for the best innovation demanded that the situation be given a fresh treatment.

Some critics have suggested that Lloyd's personality affected his work adversely—that he was too concerned with the commonplace and produced a mechanical, slick product. There may be some justification in such a view. Seldom did he venture into the land of fantasy. But neither did Keaton or Langdon. All three comedians dealt with commonplace materials. Chaplin the romantic, took a direction that appealed to many critics.

With a disposition of sunshine, Lloyd's comic character had great strength and uniqueness. So intense was this facet, it would seem that the artist had injected some of his own charm into the character. And, after interviewing Lloyd, even at this time, I believe this was the case. In some ways it may have been difficult for Lloyd to treat the serious moments in his films because he had so much optimism and gaiety. Not until I saw his 1927 *The Kid Brother* did I find a film which could evoke a great deal of sympathy for the leading comic character. In this work Lloyd was able to achieve the "pathos" often thought to be the mark of the great clown. Usually, however, those who like their clowns to have strong touches of sadness and the pathetic will not find Lloyd satisfying. Nevertheless, the sunshine of this comic portrait gives him a uniqueness among the four great silent screen comedians.

A turn now to a detailed examination of the comedian's feature films will reveal much of the skill that he possessed—a skill that made him one of the masters of comedy. Overall thematic control was an important factor in developing this quality. According to Lloyd:

> *Grandma's Boy* had told much more of a story than we ever had put in a picture before. It was a psychological study of a boy, cowardly both physically and morally, transformed by a fable invented on the spur of the moment by his despairing grandmother. . . . Before the end the boy discovers, of course, that he triumphed only because he believed in himself.[17]

This focus on a theme of regeneration would seem comic only in the manner of the genteel comedy, but Lloyd used overstatement of the boy's original weakness and overstatement of his bravery after the transformation. Thus he avoided the sentiment and the creampuff humour of the genteel tradition.

A manipulator is found in *Grandma's Boy*—a character often employed in the sentimental comedy. The "fable," mentioned above, is told to the boy to bring about his transformation. An elaborate Civil War sequence is developed by Grandma when she tells of Grandpa's spying activities for the Confederacy. (Lloyd plays a dual role in the film by taking on the character of the grandfather.) A modulation of the slapstick tradition is evident when Grandpa single-handedly defeats a group of officers engaged in a war conference. A scenario description of the comedian's method of fighting illustrates the nature of the comedy employed in this portion of the film:

> 316 MS Grandpa moves to another officer who is sitting at the table. The officer indicates that he wants another drink. He playfully punches the bogus servant in a friendly gesture of appreciation. He enjoys the potency of the drink Grandpa has mixed. Grandpa, with a broad smile, returns the friendly action with a pistol butt to the officer's head. When

the officer collapses from the blow, Grandpa puts a lily from a flower vase in the officer's hand.

For a friendly gesture, the comedian substitutes an act of aggression *as if he were being friendly*. Lloyd's smile as he deftly hits the officer provides the contrast which helps create comedy. His final touch as he places the lily in the limp hand of the officer indicates the nonchalance of the young man who fights his opponent in a perverse way. The serious profession of spying becomes a game. The comedian, in an almost childlike way, takes innocent delight in his new found ability to deal in violence.

Chaplin often employed a similar childlike behaviour when he fought an opponent. He used this attitude extensively when, as a policeman in *Easy Street* (1917), Charlie nonchalantly dropped an iron stove from a window on the head of a bully who stood in the street below. Lloyd's Grandpa in *Grandma's Boy*, on the other hand, participates in violent action with an air of innocence. His smile does not reflect the impish glee of the little tramp in Chaplin's early works. The genteel tradition obviously has some tempering effect on Lloyd's character even when he is using slapstick material.

The older tradition, however, seems to dominate in a chase sequence that leads the story to a climactic fight between the boy and his rival. It is, as Robert Sherwood points out in his review of the picture,[25] one of the most delightful portions of *Grandma's Boy*. Lloyd employs over six minutes of the film for this elaborate chase and injects a great deal of variety into this kind of much-used material. Near the end of the chase an effective comic reversal is shown.

Harold attempts to capture a tramp by driving after him in the car he has stolen. He attempts to lassoo the tramp from the automobile. Steering with one knee and sitting on the top of the front seat of the car, Harold twirls a rope above his head as a professional rodeo star would do. But his cleverness backfires. The rope misses the tramp and catches on a rural mailbox. Since the comedian has the rope tied about his waist, he is sent flying from the car with a violent jerk. Editing comes into operation in order to make this incident effective. With progressively shorter shots, from 4 seconds to $1\frac{1}{2}$ seconds, Harold is shown lassooing the mailbox instead of the tramp. This incident is accomplished in six shots which vary from long-shots to medium-shots to show the action and emphasise this comic reversal. The variety in the content of these shots, the movement, and the time of the shots assist in giving this incident vitality. It is one of the few moments in *Grandma's Boy* that show editing as a strong factor in achieving the comic. But Lloyd employs the old technique of accelerated motion during the chase sequence and generally shows good functional use of the camera to reveal or emphasise that portion of the scene which is comic.

While Lloyd, at this stage of his development, was obviously using the medium more effectively than Chaplin, he had structural problems with *Grandma's Boy*, just as Chaplin had structural problems with *The Kid*. With all its richness of humour, the Civil War sequence showing the exploits of Grandpa is disproportionately long, taking up almost eight minutes of a short, five-reel feature. It takes on some of the tangential qualities of a Chaplin film. This, however, is a fault with so many comic films. When a comedian and his writers touch upon a portion of a plot that has strong comic potentials, they are inclined to extend their inventiveness and exploit all aspects of this phase of the story. Another fault, evidently promoted by this same impulse, lies in the chase sequence. The chase reaches such a high peak of comic inventiveness and excitement that the climactic fight which follows between the rival and the boy is pale by comparison. It becomes anticlimactic. Nevertheless, the viewer's concern for the leading character's fortune and the freshness and vigour of Lloyd's acting throughout the picture hold a rather disjointed film together.

In his 1923 feature, *Safety Last*, created one year after *Grandma's Boy*, Lloyd corrected his structural faults and produced a film with an unusually tight story line. It might be called his masterpiece since it progresses so smoothly and surely. It might also be called the film which the old timers remember most, for they vividly recall Harold, the would-be human fly, clinging to the hands of a clock, with the street eleven stories below.

Like *Grandma's Boy*, *Safety Last* had the thematic concept of achievement. This theme is linked with a central comic idea based on the leading comedian's driving desire for success. This ambition makes him concoct ways of either appearing successful or becoming successful. Frequently his schemes backfire. Each reversal of fortune is an end product of his own invention. To appear successful before his girl friend, he must feign the role of a department store manager, and to carry out a publicity scheme, he must take over his friend Bill's role of a human fly. To put it simply, *Safety Last* presents the comic idea of the pretender to success who is forced to take risks that might cost him his job or even his life—a man who gets caught in the web of his own manipulations. Only his pluck, unusual ingenuity, and better than average luck save him.

The most interesting portion of the film is the climactic

sequence—a portion of the work that encompasses over a fourth of the running time. It is composed of many incidents which are clearly linked and integrated into one major action—the climb up a twelve-storey building. Each incident presents an obstacle to the comedian's laboured climb. He encounters six key obstacles in his climb: (1) pigeons, (2) a tennis net, (3) a painter's board, (4) a clock, (5) a mouse, and (6) a weather gauge. Each of these things causes successively greater danger for the comedian. The tennis net that is accidentally dropped out a window of the sports equipment section of a department store, for example, gives Harold more difficulty than the siege of overfriendly pigeons that almost makes him lose his balance. But the excitement which seems to aid in developing the comedy is not the only factor at work. The comedian's struggle with this obstacle also becomes more outlandish—more laughable. He struggles with the net in a dance-like fashion; he slips it from his head only to have it catch on an arm or leg. The routine is reminiscent of the circus clown's bout with sticky taffy or flypaper. In this case, though, the routine has the added excitement of the danger that is created by this dance of frustration on a narrow ledge above a city street.

Visual humour in this sequence is punctuated with verbal comic remarks from onlookers. The understatement of the title "Why don'tcha take the net off? It's in your way!" assists the pantomime. An elderly lady is shown standing at a window in the building, scolding the would-be human fly by saying "Young man, don't you know you might fall and get hurt?" Again, the comic understatement of the title adds variety and counterpoint to a situation which deals in overstatement.

Harold, throughout his whole ordeal, attempts to fulfil his obligations as a performer by acknowledging the crowd with a broad smile, but the smile becomes tighter as the danger increases. His face becomes twisted with comic horror when the famous clock incident is enacted. He slips from the window and grabs frantically at the edge of the huge clock on the corner of the Bolton Building that shows the time of two forty-five. He cannot hold on to the edge of the clock but clutches the big hand and, horror of horrors, the hand moves down with his weight to half past two. As Harold attempts to pull himself up by grabbing the small hand, the crowning blow of this incident occurs—the whole face of the clock springs outward and down. The complications do not stop at this stage, however. His companion, Bill, throws Harold a rope which hangs just out of reach. The audience viewing the film is informed that Bill, frightened away by a policeman, has not tied the rope to the leg of an office desk as he had intended. A close-up provides this information with sharp impact. In the next shot Harold is shown desperately trying to reach the rope. Then, as he grabs the rope, Bill returns just in time to snatch the other end of the rope before it flies over the window sill. Since this last second rescue employs accelerated motion, Bill's unusually fast dive for the rope is placed on a superhuman and comic level.

This situation reaches the fantastic proportions of an early Mack Sennett one-reel comedy. It is an incident which fans its comic fire with the unusual and the impossible. The last-second rescue shows the use of overstatement. A close-up of Harold's face as he dangles on the end of the rope supports the comic nature of this highly dangerous situation. His expression is one of wild horror; his eyes pop behind shell-rimmed glasses. Each action and reaction shot emphasises the situation and promotes comic overstatement.

When it would appear that Harold has reached the top of the

building and is, at last, safe, he encounters the final obstacle as he crawls over the top ledge. He stands up and is nearly knocked unconscious by a wind gauge. Dizzy from the blow, he staggers along the top ledge of the building in a drunk-like dance, teetering backward and forward.

The final spectacular predicament develops from this staggering pantomime. The comedian's foot catches in the rope of a flag pole, and he is hurled out head first in a pendulum swing over the city street twelve stories below. The full force of the medium comes into play to assist the staging of this spectacular finish. Editing takes over to produce the desired illusion:

> 764 LS A double for Harold Lloyd is shown swinging by his ankle next to the building in a pendulum-like swing to left frame from the right. (4 seconds).
> 765 MLS The flag pole alone is shown as it bends with the swing to the right and back to the left. (3 seconds).
> 766 LS "Harold" is shown in another swing to the right and back toward the left. (4 seconds).
> 767 LS Mildred stands on the roof of the building with outstretched arms. Harold swings up to the ledge on the rope and falls into her arms. They embrace. ($1\frac{1}{2}$ seconds).

This fantastic finish to this well conceived and well executed sequence indicates the extent to which Lloyd and his directors had mastered the techniques of cinema in 1923. A trained observer of the motion pictures can detect the fact that the majority of shots showing Harold outside the building were staged with motion picture sets (unlike *Grandma's Boy* in which the entire climactic sequence was shot with "actualities" on location), while some long-shots of the climb showed a double, a professional human fly, climbing a real building. According to the *Literary Digest* of July, 1923, a dummy structure of a building was constructed on the roof of a real building in order to provide the necessary illusion. The proper camera angles were also used to provide the illusion of height.[58] In his autobiography, Lloyd points out that this same method was employed for the one-, two-, and three-reel comedies of this genre.[17]

But Lloyd did not depend on this type of spectacular material alone. The audience viewing the picture needed to become involved with the fortunes of this young man. He developed his character by using simple material. Earlier in the film, he desired to see his boss but obviously didn't have the courage to meet him face to face. Lloyd executed a brilliant piece of pantomime from very routine story material. The camera remained at a neutral, medium-shot position as an interesting step by step study in comic anxiety developed:

> 548 MS Harold starts to knock on the General Manager's door and, in a continuous motion of his hand, turns the direction of his knock into a grasp at his collar.
>
> He returns to his task of entering once more. He moves his hand to the door but stops it short and hesitatingly touches the frame of the door rather than the door itself.
>
> Screwing up his courage, he starts to knock again. His hand swings in the air three times without hitting the door. He moves his hand up to the back of his head and down his face in a frustrated manner.
>
> He steps back and gathers up his courage with his fist poised in the air, but his courage withers

> and he puts his hands in his pockets and walks a few nervous steps away from the door.
>
> Gathering what is left of his manhood, he approaches the door with the determined pose of a fighter—both fists extended. Both hands start to knock but end up waving limply in the air. Harold nearly collapses from anxiety and leans against the door. The door opens from his weight. Horrified, he grabs it to keep it from opening any farther.

This incident is a brilliant *tour de force*. The pantomime is executed with a skill that illustrates the reason Harold Lloyd created a place in the sun beside the strong competition of the master pantomimist, Charles Chaplin. His routine is interestingly developed by a variation on one action which builds to sharp reversals. He shows his comic character exerting a great deal of effort which ends up in inactivity.

Lloyd did not always develop his comic portrait as effectively as he did in *Grandma's Boy* and *Safety Last*. His *Doctor Jack* and *Why Worry?* in 1923 and his *Girl Shy* and *Hot Water* contain slight character development. These works rely more on farcical situations and do not have the strong thematic development that gave strength to his best films. *The Freshman* in 1925, however, shows Lloyd returning to his former working method.

In theme and comic idea *The Freshman* and *Grandma's Boy* share similar characteristics. Both deal with a young man's desire for social acceptance. The earlier work, *Grandma's Boy*, depends on a comic idea which shows a sharp inversion of a man's behaviour, turning him from the attributes of a coward to those of a hero. *The Freshman* demands an inversion of the character called Harold Lamb, but the shift in behaviour or attitude comes from a social group and not from the leading character. In this work Harold succeeds (despite an outrageous display of incompetence as a football player) and is acclaimed a hero by his peers. He has saved the day and is accepted. As in *Grandma's Boy*, this work plays with the idea of the hero on a comic level. It is not outstanding skill that makes either the character of Boy or Harold Lamb heroes; it is an almost manic drive for success coupled with luck that pushes both characters from a low state in their associates' eyes to a high level of social acceptance.

While *The Freshman* does not have the structural perfection of *Safety Last*, it contains Lloyd's best use of the motion picture medium for comedy effects. The stock pratfall, for example, is refurbished and clearly pointed up with the assistance of the medium. When the comic protagonist, Harold Lamb, tries to rescue a small cat that is marooned on a high spot by climbing onto a speaker's stand, his improvised ladder begins to teeter back and forth. The action is first shown in a long-shot—then:

> 137 MS Harold sways on the pedestal. He tips backwards and then from side to side.

In this shot, a closer view is given to emphasise Harold's plight. The long-shot which follows catches the broad action of the fall:

> 138 LS He falls (toward frame left) and twists backward as he crashes to the floor.

And then, a quick cut to another closer view shows the results:

> 139 MS Harold sprawls back over his luggage on the stage floor. He pulls out his ukulele from behind him—it is shattered.

When Harold tries to become a football hero, he is given the trying task of substituting for a broken tackle dummy during football practice. The correct angle by the camera creates one of the highest comic moments in this laugh provoking sequence:

> 380 LS Harold rises to his knees. He finally gets up, staggers, and reels like a drunken man. He falls flat on his back.
>
> 381 MS He starts to get up. He appears to have both legs extended as he finally gets up on one knee. To the right and behind him lies the dummy which has lost a leg. Harold's left leg seems to extend forward as if it were grotesquely twisted out of joint. Harold looks down at his leg, horrified at the sight. He grabs what he thinks is his leg and finds it free, as if his leg were unhinged by an injury. Dazed, he sits back and pulls the left leg which is, in reality, safely bent under him. The loose leg before him is, of course, the dummy's leg which has previously been torn off in tackling practice. Relieved to find this out, Harold crawls off.

As Arthur Knight points out, the above incident illustrates the use of a particular camera angle whereby the shot may display the comedian's leg as if it were a "grotesquely broken leg."[15] This shot does even more than Knight indicates. The audience might share the comedian's interpretation if the camera angle did not also reveal the tackle dummy minus one leg in the background.

With the same skill he exhibits in all his works, Lloyd incorporates a clean-cut, logical method of building toward the funniest material in the final sequences of *The Freshman.* A series of embarrassments with a faulty tuxedo at a party leads to

The progress of Harold Lamb (Lloyd) in the 1925 THE FRESHMAN towards success on the football field.

Top left: a Lloyd gag from THE FRESHMAN (1925) showing the comic character mistaking a tackle dummy's leg for his own. Below left: Lloyd tried to avoid the old gag of losing his pants in THE FRESHMAN but a preview indicated that the genteel act of shedding a coat was not enough. Lloyd reshot the scene as shown in this frame enlargement with some refurbishing of the ancient gag. Right: MAD WEDNESDAY (also called THE SIN OF HAROLD DIDDLEBOCK) was the last film comedy to star Harold Lloyd. It employed an opening scene from THE FRESHMAN to introduce the story.

Harold Lamb's eventual loss of his pants. While this is a gag as old as comedy itself (Lloyd worried about the "old hat" nature of the gag), it is carefully motivated and the comic disaster is executed with exceptionally good taste. Lloyd also works up a fine chain of gags burlesquing the last minute touchdown that was handled by the solo performance of the hero in so many of the slick, serious movies of the Twenties. This provides the climactic portion of the drama—a sequence that lasts eighteen minutes of this six-reel feature. No finer film burlesque of the college hero has been made.

A close look at Lloyd's use of character in his works shows that plot and character are strongly integrated. Even though he has used many strong situation gags which stand out, and has produced comic incidents which seem to be based more on situation than character, the importance of the leading character is evident throughout the work. Lloyd uses character as the basis of plot development.

The key to understanding the comic character created by Lloyd lies in the leading figure's zeal. The enthusiasm of this character gives it distinction. Leading comedians of the time, Chaplin, Keaton, and Langdon, seldom used this trait in their comic characters. Lloyd, on the other hand, uses this trait as the basic facet of his portrait. Some of the best comic moments of his films occur when Harold's zeal leads him into situations which backfire. In *Safety Last*, Harold is forced to live two roles—one to impress his girl that he is a success, and the other to maintain his position as a lowly clerk in a department store. His desire to make a promotional stunt succeed forces him to assume the role of a human fly. Throughout *The Freshman*, Harold Lamb's eagerness to be socially accepted makes him a fool in the eyes of the people he is trying to impress. He becomes a ridiculous figure because he attempts feats he is ill-equipped to handle; he tries to make a speech before the student body, and he struggles pathetically to play the game of football. In *Grandma's Boy*, his enthusiasm to display his courage backfires many times as he pursues the tramp. In each case, however, the fault that gains laughter is also the virtue that wins the victory. Victory is achieved, it must be pointed out, with the assistance of luck.

In an attempt to gain more sympathy for his protagonist, Lloyd unfortunately is not so successful in blending serious and comic materials as Chaplin and Langdon were. Serious incidents are introduced momentarily in Lloyd's works when Boy in *Grandma's Boy* and Harold Lamb in *The Freshman* break down and weep. These moments are not effectively handled; there is not the underplaying of the serious situation which made Chaplin and Langdon successful. There are moments, however, in which Lloyd captures the audience with a blend of the serious and the comic. In the early part of *Grandma's Boy*, the plight of Boy when he is pushed into a well by his rival is effectively played. Also a touch of tender comedy results from Harold Lamb's mauling by team-mates when he is forced to assume the role of a tackle dummy for football practice. Dazed by this gruelling punishment, the young man collapses wearily on the shoulders of the coach who has given him the assignment. Pathetically, he slides to the feet of the coach and, like a faithful dog, remains devoted to his master who glares unsympathetically down at him. It is one of Lloyd's best blendings of the serious and the comic.

In the final analysis, Lloyd's portrait seems more firmly planted in the genteel tradition of comedy. However, his character moves in an unusual world in which many things can happen. He can encounter situations that force him to fight, climb a tall building, or chase an outlaw. In such moments, broad, slapstick comedy seems to reign. In the shadows of the most frenzied activity that grips this character, however, lies the basic sentimentalised concept. He is the young man striving to get ahead. Some of his setbacks, the milder moments of his films, reveal the genteel comic character in embarrassments that are too tame for the slapstick tradition. But he undergoes a rapid metamorphosis in dire circumstances—then, only a hint of the genteel character remains; nevertheless, it is always there. When Lloyd's protagonist struggles the hardest (a trait in the genteel tradition), many of the facets of the older clown overshadow the new one—the slapstick character of the past springs forth in full bloom.

5. An Eye on the Horizon

WHILE Buster Keaton is probably the silent comedian best known to this generation—because of his appearances in television commercials, variety shows, and such series programmes as *Route 66* and *The Greatest Show on Earth*, few young people today have seen films starring this great comedian at the height of his creative powers. In his present day efforts there remained only a flicker of the greatness that was his in the Twenties. Keaton appeared as a has-been. Unfortunately his writers in television shows tried to bestow upon him the Chaplinesque "pathos" of the sad, soul-struck Pierrot—a comic tone with which they evidently had only a nodding acquaintance since Keaton's character, in their hands, often became saccharine and too sentimental.

The vigour of Keaton in his heyday was far removed from sentimentality. His little clown was a struggling, dead-panned dunce who looked to the horizon, Indian fashion, like an automaton of steel that could not be crushed by a train, hurricane, or avalanche. But this agile, mechanical doll struggled doggedly, often swinging by his teeth and fingernails, to fight the obstacle that confronted him; and he won by weird, comic ingenuity. Passions known to man—especially love and hate—flickered faintly in the creature's make-up. While the head and heart functioned feebly, the body could assume leonine aggression and determination. Here was a dauntless, acrobatic manikin with a sad yet blank face confronting the world with a body bent forward against the wheel of fortune.

There were many facets in Keaton's off-stage personality that affected his films. Since his dunce-clown was uncannily convincing, some people, especially producers, thought the actor might have the same simple, uncomplicated personality. Sometimes he played that role because, like many people, he attempted to fulfil the image attributed to him. But inside Buster was a bright man—a bundle of energy, innovation and sensitivity. During a crisis he clasped the mask tightly over his true emotions; sometimes he seemed to be as anaesthetised from life as the famous character he portrayed on the screen.

Even when he was in vaudeville with his father and mother in an act billed as "The Three Keatons," Buster was a hard worker. As a child star he was thrown about—upset and tumbled—in a comic "knock-about" act. To get the best gags from their act, father and son practised long and hard.

At an early age, between 13 and 14, Buster relished practical jokes and showed considerable skill in rigging up embarrassing Rube Goldberg gags to catch unwary guests in the Keaton home. Rudi Blesh's penetrating study mentions many of the inventions of the young actor who had become more successful in vaudeville than his parents so that he got more attention and top billing in their act.[2]

Keaton produced his intriguing comedies in the Twenties with much of his obsession for gadgets assisting him in the creation. Many of his two-reel films and his features focused on machines. In *Our Hospitality* (1923) and *The General* (1926) the locomotive seemed to become a co-actor; and *The Navigator* (1924) had an ocean liner that could have stolen scenes from Keaton if the comedian hadn't been so closely enmeshed with "the machine."

More than the other major comedians, Keaton wanted authentic locales, costumes, and props in the execution of his stories. This is especially evident in his works, *Our Hospitality* and *The General*, two of his most important features set in a past age. And while it would seem to be a personality trait of being too concerned with realistic detail that might work against the comic spirit, Keaton was able to make his type of realism work in his favour. The authentic tone of the past actually provided a milieu for the abstraction and overstatement necessary for comedy. At times there was even a fascinating counterpart to our present day attitudes that helped promote the humour.

No thorough analysis of Keaton's personality and the way it affected his works can overlook his attitude toward acrobatic gags. He was surely the superior comic in this activity (with Lloyd running a close second) and was daring in executing some of the most spectacular comic tricks of all times. In his early days he padded himself and doubled for Fatty Arbuckle—executed a fall from a train and a long tumble down the side of a hill, rolling into the door of a saloon. His daring verged on the fantastic. Many of his co-workers thought he was stupid or insane to have the two-ton front of a house collapse over him like a giant fly swatter in *Steamboat Bill, Jr.* (1927) with only a three inch clearance around his shoulders of an open window to prevent him from being crushed to death. He also took his life in his hands many times as he scampered over a locomotive in *The General*. But all this risk was necessary according to Keaton's fearless view of creating the comic thrill. There seemed no length to which he would not go in order to get such strong spice into his pictures.

Unfortunately, Keaton's artistic integrity was not linked with a strong business sense. Chaplin and Lloyd had a combination of these qualities that helped them retain control of their productions and kept the merit of their films on a high level until nearly the end of their careers. Late in the Twenties Keaton's films began to wane in quality when he lost control of the total creative process. In his autobiography a chapter entitled "The Worst Mistakes of My Life" tells how he was pitted against the big business system of M-G-M. The mistake was giving up his own company and letting M-G-M control his total production of comedy films. Somewhat oversimplifying his plight, he wrote that the craftsmen in his production unit "behaved like prima donnas":

> Having less to gain through pleasing me than men on my team would, they were often more interested in getting outstanding results for their specialty instead of co-operating fully to get the story told in the quickest way possible. Not being on a team they rarely forgot that their next assignment depended on their work standing out, instead of being subordin-

ated to the excellence of the picture as a whole. Under M-G-M's system each craftsman was more beholden to the head of his department than to me.[14]

While this was a manifestation, it was not the cause of the comedian's decline. Rudi Blesh does an excellent job of evaluating Keaton's weakness in business arrangements—the root of his trouble in the late Twenties. He was obsessed with his art even in the early days of one- and two-reel productions with Joe Schenck. Financial matters didn't interest him:

> These details, Buster Keaton quite evidently thought, lay outside the serious pursuit of laughter. They were offstage entirely. He gave hardly a thought to the business aspects of his new situation. While Schenck was explaining them, Buster had barely listened, his mind already far ahead planning new routines on a new stage.[2]

And regarding the unusual paternal organisation in which he was entangled even in the early Twenties, Blesh states:

> It was so much Buster Keaton's native pattern that he never thought to question whether such an anomaly belonged or could long last in the fierce, competitive movie world. The assembly lines were then being laid out in the cinema factories. In the customary American hocus-pocus—or "ledger-domain"—tradition, an art was being subverted into a business with jungle ethics.[2]

In short, Keaton, like Harry Langdon, was a babe in the woods when it came to the business world. When Keaton was allowed nearly complete control of his art, he did excellent work. Therefore, it would seem that Lloyd was the only comedian of first-rate ability that could co-operate with the system and still produce quality films. Chaplin, with the aid of his brother Sidney, remained untouched. He enjoyed a rare private domain in the world of Hollywood since he linked himself with United Artists, teaming up with two other greats of the period, Douglas Fairbanks and Mary Pickford.

As one of the four leading comedians of the silent age of cinema, Keaton was the only one that didn't work for Mack Sennett. In 1917 he was a successful vaudeville comedian, receiving $250 a week for his comic acrobatics. Roscoe ("Fatty") Arbuckle urged him to enter the movies for $40 per week; but he was able to work up to his vaudeville salary in a year.[14]

His early two-reel works with Arbuckle were of little critical worth, but Keaton became a popular success. He learned the skills of acting, directing, editing, and story composition for the medium from Arbuckle. Little critical success can be claimed for his first acting role in a long work. His first feature, *The Saphead* (1920) showed very little of the skill that was to make him an object of critical acclaim. The basic material used for this film was Bronson Howard's satirical melodrama on business, *The Henrietta*, a work created in 1887 for the Broadway theatre. Keaton was not closely tied to the production aspects of this picture but he had attained the stature of co-star with the famous stage actor, William H. Greene.

When Keaton was able to strike out on his own with two-reelers for Metro Pictures Corporation in 1920, he started his climb to both popular and critical acclaim. His 1921 two-reel work, *The Paleface*, was a forecast of a bright future. Keaton and Eddie Cline had formed a writing and directing team that was to bring out the best in the comedian and prepare him for his excellent feature films of the middle Twenties.

Somewhat thin in plot material, *The Paleface* nevertheless

exhibits the type of inventive gags that Keaton was to employ in his feature pictures. A title introduces the comic character as Jack Kee "courageously pursuing his game" in Indian territory. The comedian peeks around a stockade gate and then pulls his butterfly net into view. A revelation gag is executed by the actor in this instance; Keaton was later to use the camera to advantage to embellish and enforce this type of joke.

Captured by Indians, Buster stoically pulls up the stake to which he has been tied and moves a few feet away just after an Indian has piled wood at his feet. The Indian is perplexed and moves the wood next to the bound man. Buster's repetition of this same movement sends the Indian into a nervous breakdown. Escaping from the frustrated Indian by bending forward and knocking him out with the pole to which he is tied, Buster climbs down the chimney of a pioneer's cabin and fashions himself an undergarment of asbestos paper. After a brief chase he is once more captured by the Indians and tied to the stake; a huge fire seems to consume him. The smoke clears and Buster is revealed with his outer suit burned to shreds and his soot covered face looking blankly at the Indians who stand around him in amazement. They prostrate themselves before him as if he were a god. Nonchalantly, Buster looks for a match to light a cigarette; he finds a smouldering stick underfoot and lights it. As a substitute peace pipe, the chief of the tribe is offered a puff from the cigarette.

What may be considered Keaton's first masterpiece appeared the following year—1922. *Cops*, another two-reeler by the Eddie Cline and Buster Keaton team, displays a strong story line with excellent camera technique and editing—a work replete with original gags. The opening shots predate Harold Lloyd's use of a similar gag in *Safety Last* (1923). Buster is shown behind bars speaking to his girl friend who appears to be outside a prison. The next shot, a long-shot, reveals that the comic character is merely saying goodbye to a girl who lives in a huge mansion surrounded by an iron fence with bars, much like those used in jails.

Endeavouring to become a businessman to please his wealthy girl friend, Buster gets an old horse and wagon for any type of business venture. A con man sells him a mountain of furniture that belongs to an off-duty policeman who is waiting for a mover to take his belongings to a new house that he has purchased.

The whole film turns into a comic, unintentional assault on policemen. Buster "steals" the furniture, hits a policeman while driving his loaded wagon, and breaks up an elaborate policemen's parade by innocently moving his vehicle into the middle of the pomp and ceremony. While this type of deflating of dignity and authority can be traced to the Sennett tradition, there is a very different tone to the whole development and execution of the gags. Broad, unmotivated slapstick seldom intrudes. The film progresses clearly and cleanly in a series of logical, unintentional assaults on stuffy policemen. No well-placed whacks with clubs or bricks in the style of the wildly mischievous little tramps that were pursued by the Keystone Cops mar this minor masterpiece. Keaton followed Lloyd and many of the polite comedians by hanging in the attic many of the stock gimmicks of the 1910's that he had used while working with Fatty Arbuckle. Later, in 1924, he expressed his view on the older slapstick devices: "A comedian today no longer finds his dressing room filled with slapstick property bricks, stuffed clubs and exploding cigars. Comic situations have taken the place of these veteran laugh getters."[12]

While Keaton overstates his rejection of the stock devices—some of the old gimmicks, slightly refurbished, pop up from time to time in his films—he has put aside the spirit of the off-the-cuff, helter-skelter slapstick film of Mack Sennett. Keaton's story is fresh, sharp, and straightforward; each incident triggers another and leads to a logical conclusion. Even the chase undergoes a metamorphosis in tone. It burlesques the chase by having the hapless clown pursued by a whole city's police force after Buster is falsely blamed for intentionally throwing a bomb into the policemen's parade. His varied ways of eluding the pursuers reveal Keaton's comic invention and acrobatic skill. Especially effective is Keaton's nonchalant pose as he stands on a street corner after he has outstripped an army of cops. With a mechanical, deft lift of one arm he catches ahold of the back of a passing truck and is whisked off, his heels flying parallel with the cobblestones.

Cops has one similarity to Charles Chaplin's *Easy Street* (1917). Chaplin was never able to obtain the same unified progression in his feature works as he was in this well constructed two-reeler. Likewise, Keaton could never achieve the same tight, well-knit development in his features. Keaton, however, showed much greater skill in unifying his works than Chaplin, but like Chaplin he was often guilty of digression from the main progression of the story.

In an otherwise successful film, *Our Hospitality* (1923), Keaton's second independently conceived feature,* disunity and disproportionment reign. The opening sequence repeats the error of Chaplin's *The Kid* (1921) by beginning the film as if it

*A six-reel work, *The Three Ages,* was released in September, a month before *Our Hospitality.* Of the two *Our Hospitality* was considered by the critics to be the best work.

were a serious treatment of a serious theme. Writing for potential screen authors, Scott O'Dell dismisses this weakness by rationalising: "The story has a somewhat melodramatic prologue, starting as it does with a double murder. However, the student should not allow himself to become confused regarding the necessity for using this prologue. It is the consensus of opinion that the use of a prologue is poor technique; but in this case it seems justifiable, as it is much more effective than would be a retrospect."[20]

While there is some truth in O'Dell's observation, the comic mood of the film, as in Chaplin's *The Kid*, is not established until later in the development of the story; and in both works the comedians have a longer climb uphill to establish laughter.

Keaton also seems to err in a disproportionate concern with the comic potentialities of an old train—as a result, the main conflict of the plot, a feud between two families, and all the comedy that springs from it, must wait until a third of the picture has gone by.

With the next picture, *Sherlock, Jr.*, released in April 1924, Keaton produced one of his best works. Its plot development, drawing of comedy character, and imaginative comic incidents place it among the greatest screen comedies of all times.

One imaginative, short sequence in the film stands out as the moment that everyone remembers. All critics who viewed it when the picture was first released, as well as those who see it today, were struck by the "cinematic" comedy created by Keaton in the early portion of the dream sequence. In scenario form this unusual, brief portion of the work runs as follows:

> 124 MS Buster, sleeping in the motion picture projection booth with his head on his arms, twitches as if disturbed.

125 ELS The dream Buster goes up to the side of the movie screen stage and steps up next to the picture that is being projected on a huge screen.
126 ELS The frame changes on the movie screen to show the front of a mansion. Buster jumps *into* the picture. He looks around, puzzled by the environment that he has penetrated. The Father comes out the door and down a few steps.
127 LLS (slightly closer than the extreme-long-shot) Forgetting something, the Father goes back into the house. Buster runs up the steps and knocks on the door. No response. He turns and starts down the steps. . . .
128 LLS . . . the frame changes and Buster steps on a bench in a garden scene and tumbles over on his head and shoulders. He gets up and looks around with a puzzled shake of his body; he starts to sit down on the bench. . . .
129 LLS . . . and he falls from a sitting position into the street that is busy with scurrying people and speeding cars. He gets up and jumps quickly from the street onto a kerb as an automobile almost hits him. He ducks and scampers back off the kerb as two pedestrians walking side by side nearly bump into him. He goes left then decides to go right. . . .
130 LLS . . . and finds himself in a contrasting environment. He is walking on rough mountain terrain. Suddenly he realises he has nearly walked off the edge of a precipice—he teeters, waving his hands violently to keep his balance—then falls down, clutching the rock from which he has slipped. He gets up and looks back (right) over the edge. . . .
131 LLS . . . and the frame changes with Buster

looking down at the ground in the middle of an African jungle A lion stirs in the background. Cautiously Buster moves left. . . .
132 LLS . . . the frame changes and he discovers himself in the middle of a desert. He moves back toward the centre. Seeing something off right he scurries forward and dives into a large hole in the sand. A trains roars by from right frame and off left frame. Buster gets up and kicks the sand in frustration. He looks briefly around with his hand to his forehead in Indian fashion. He wearily sits on the sand. . . .
133 LLS . . . and the frame changes. He is now sitting on a rock with huge waves beating around and over him. In desperation he dives. . . .
134 LLS . . . . not into the ocean but into a snowbank, for the frame has switched on him again. He is upended, his head sticking in the snow, his feet kicking. Finally, he gets up on his feet, puts his hands disgustedly and wearily on his hips. Then he starts to lean against a small tree. . . .
135 LLS . . . and falls into the garden scene once more. He does a backward somersault and ends up on his stomach.

While this skilfully worked out "cinematic" segment may seem contrived when it is written in scenario form, the acrobatics of Keaton save it from self-consciousness in the film. All movements are adroitly handled—the nightmare of the blank-faced little clown becomes a comic ballet of the film. A laughable, surrealistic world of the cinema promotes unique, original comedy. I know of no film of the Twenties that exploits so extensively and successfully the editing principles of the medium.

Interestingly enough, this brief episode also shows Keaton executing his Indian style survey of the horizon—a gesture that he used in most of his films. This attitude becomes symbolic. The poor dunce is often shown lost in a broad, unknown, hostile world. Furthermore, the total sequence might be considered the epitome of the plight of the little clown that Keaton creates. As one unnamed reviewer phrased it, Keaton is the "Humpty Dumpty of the screen . . . always falling from the wall and always getting up again."[56]

But this aspect of Keaton's film dramas is only a portion of the total picture. Historians Bardèche and Brasillach try to reduce his comedy to this outstanding facet by stating: "Keaton really became a relatively abstract personality, a mathematician highly gifted in calculating laughter."[1] Christopher Bishop makes the same error of reduction by stating that the comic character created by Keaton "seems detached from his surroundings, uninvolved to the point of lunacy, an extraordinarily neutral figure, driven by compulsion beyond his comprehension, his behaviour without source in any conscious motivation."[28]

Such evaluations of Keaton's character are quite common and they are intended as penetrating views on the essence of Keaton's comedy. They fail to take into account many of the particular comic character facets that are advanced in the development of the drama. In *Sherlock Jr.*, for example, there are many of the obsessed young boy characteristics that are quite fundamental to the plot and not "abstract" or lacking in "conscious motivation." Granted, Keaton creates the village dimwit who is hardly capable of being a motion picture projectionist, but he endows him with childish enthusiasm for the life of a famous detective. In his dream world, the comic protagonist acts with deliberation and amazing skill as he pits his unusual talents against the crime world. In reality, of course, the young man is incapable of solving a simple crime—his girl friend has more skill at sleuthing than he has. Nevertheless, the character has some resemblance to the small town boy who is trying to make good. Basically, Keaton seems to be employing some of the same type of material Harold Lloyd used. This film, as well as other Keaton works, depends on such story material and characterisation. In *Sherlock, Jr.*, his comic character has a bit of Lloyd's character's determination. He shadows his rival in love regardless of any obstacle that comes into his pathway. But unlike Lloyd's character, he endows his character with classic stupidity. In this respect his character is similar to Harry Langdon's and Stan Laurel's.

Keaton also displays another similarity to Lloyd in his method of story composition and character development. He changes some facets of his characterisation (and consequently, his plot development) from picture to picture. Following the release of *Sherlock, Jr.*, Keaton came out the same year (1924) with *The Navigator* and changed his character from a poor young man to a rich young man. While the change may seem superficial, it is not. Keaton makes a great deal of comedy out of the fact that this rich, spoiled boob cannot do anything for himself in the early portions of the film and is later forced to change his ways when he is cast adrift on a huge ocean liner with only his girl to assist him in his plight.

In *The Navigator* Keaton was less successful in developing a unified work. *Sherlock, Jr.*, a five-reel feature, moved surely and directly through the use of a strong-willed dream character, the "Sherlock, Jr." of the film. This dream episode forms the largest and most interesting portion of the film. The basic situa-

Two studies of Buster Keaton. That at left is from a 1921 two-reel comedy THE PALEFACE.

Three shots from SHERLOCK, JR. (1924). In the opening (at right) Buster finds it hard to concentrate on his job because of his dreams of an exciting profession. The book is 'How To Be a Detective'. Below left: in the elaborate dream sequence, Buster and his girl accidentally go adrift in a car that floats. Below right: a rare serious moment in a Keaton film when the little man is given back his engagement ring.

tion, the obsession of the young man in the real world, imparts strength to the plot development. Even before Buster becomes the superman sleuth of fantasy, the plot is moving rapidly and interestingly forward. By contrast, the comic protagonist of *The Navigator,* a rich, pampered young man named Rollo Treadway, does not have a similar obsession which promotes plot development. At the beginning of the story he is obviously lacking in drive. As if he were going to buy a new suit, he tells his valet that he is going to get married; he marches mechanically up to a young woman who is a friend of the family and states unemotionally: "Will you marry me?" She instantly and vehemently replies, "Certainly not!" Rollo looks blankly away from her, turns on his heels, takes his cane and hat from a servant, and leaves the girl without another word spoken.

While Keaton achieves comedy from this type of character, he does not assist the progression of the story with it until his young man is forced to take action after being cast adrift at sea. The fumbling, sometimes futile efforts of the ordinarily idle young man and girl to cook a meal and feed themselves for survival produce excellent comedy. Rollo creates many Rube Goldberg devices to cook the meals in a galley of pots, pans, and utensils that were designed to feed an army of ocean liner passengers. Rollo pulls a lever, and a steel arm with a single match on it strikes, lights, and starts a fire in the coal-burning stove; his girl friend pulls a lever, and coffee grounds slide down a trough into a huge coffee pot. In order to boil eggs in a monstrous pot, Rollo dips a rat cage containing eggs into the steaming water.

While most of the camerawork is routine and utilitarian, the position of the camera assists greatly in developing one of the better gags of the picture. At the urgings of his girl friend, Rollo gets into a rowing boat and ties a rope to the enormous ocean liner. An extreme-long-shot shows how ridiculous and diminutive his efforts are as he tries to tow the great ship. The shot shows the whole ship and a speck of a rowing boat before its bow. The comic effect: a flea trying to pull an elephant by the trunk.

In a climactic fight with natives who board the ship and try to capture the castaways, Keaton executes one of the best gags of the picture—a joke that he refurbished for *The General* (1927). He lights a small signal cannon in this battle with the islanders and accidentally gets his foot entangled in the rope attached to the weapon. He frantically scurries away from the cannon, but it remains pointed squarely at him regardless of his gyrations and the objects he tries to hide behind. As a savage with spear in hand plunges toward him, Rollo ducks, and the cannon shoots squarely into the native's chest and face. Keaton handles this incident masterfully. His frantic scampering is an artful, funny dance of fear and frustration.

Despite some of these effective routines and individual gags, the film needs trimming. About one reel could be eliminated from the picture in order to cut over-extended routines. The logic of the work's development is sketchy and often relies on chance happenings. The climactic struggle with the natives is not forecast or prepared for in any way. Probably the greatest weakness lies in the film's lack of direct conflict of the type used in *Our Hospitality* and *The General*. The struggles for survival on board the ship are short lived and are solved without a great deal of effort by the comic character's unusual ingenuity. Keaton considered it one of his favourite films,[28] but it leaves much to be desired. *Sherlock, Jr.*, *The General*, and *Our Hospitality* are considerably better comedies.

Keaton's 1927 feature, *The General*, as it has been indicated, has the virtue of a very strong conflict. Like *Sherlock, Jr.*, the comic character has a strong obsession which promotes plot development of an intense, clear-cut nature. In the opening sequence of the film, direct title narration points out that Johnny Gray (Keaton's character) has two loves in his life—his engine (the locomotive called "The General") and his girl friend, Annabelle Lee. The viewer of this film soon realises which object of Johnny's affections is best loved. When Union spies steal his locomotive, of which he is engineer, he exerts herculean efforts to recover the stolen machine from the camp of the enemy.

The novel feature of this film lies in its elaboration of the heretofore confined chase sequence. While many features of the Twenties employed the chase sequence as the climactic portion of the picture, the bulk of this film comedy's material revolves around two extensive, detailed chases. One chase by Johnny is to recover the locomotive from the Union army, and the other concerns his escape from enemy territory in "The General." On the other hand, the climactic sequences use a spectacular battle between two armies. Herein lies the basic weakness of the work. The chase portion is excellently conceived and executed, but the battle episode becomes anti-climactic. According to the logic of the story, the battle *should* be the climax. At the beginning of the film, Johnny has been rejected from military service because he is a locomotive engineer and is needed by the Confederation to work in the war effort. Johnny feels he must be a war hero but is frustrated by this rejection. However, his obsession for "The General's" safety becomes the main obsession of the film during the chase portions. Such an emphasis evolves so effectively that it becomes the main part of the story line—it is paramount, and all else becomes superfluous. The battle becomes an appendix tacked onto an otherwise skilfully developed story.

Despite this weakness, *The General* has many excellent situations and gags. An incident similar to that used in *The Navigator* develops when Johnny, standing on a moving train, tries to fire a cannon at the Union army. As sole pursuer who is trying to captain a locomotive and fire a huge cannon, he displays his unusual, sometimes bungling talents. He seems more like a child playing the game of war. He loads and lights the bulky, stubby-nosed weapon and starts to climb back to the fuel car of the engine. His foot gets hooked in the linkage between the cars, and the flat car supporting the cannon jolts on a bumpy track in such a fashion that the weapon's barrel moves down on its swivel and points directly at the hapless little fellow. Johnny finally frees himself and vainly throws a couple of small sticks of wood at the cannon. He climbs to the very front of the train and shudders on the cowcatcher, expecting the worst. A curve in the tracks saves him, and the shell from the cannon whizzes past the frightened engineer and explodes in an embankment ahead of the train.

Throughout the chase scenes, the dauntless Keaton shows effective comic ingenuity as he either removes booby traps in front of him when he is the pursuer or leaves obstacles behind him when he is being pursued. He jumps about manning the locomotive like a busy squirrel gathering nuts. And, symbolically, at one point in the pursuit, he climbs on the cab of the train and looks, Indian fashion, at the world before him.

A great deal of comedy is achieved by showing the frustration of the Union army generals as they are outmanoeuvred by the obstacles that dimwitted Johnny puts in their way. For his final blow to the train pursuing him, he sets a bridge on fire. One general consults another and asks if the bridge is too badly burned to cross. The seemingly wise general on horseback declares: "That bridge is not burned enough to stop you; and my men will ford the river." The Union train chugs across; the colossal blunder becomes apparent when the bridge gives way and the whole train plunges into the river.

Most of the gags which I have explored in this analysis of *The General* are on the grand scale. This is one of the main distinctions of this comic film. It is comedy in an epic style. No other comedy of this time ventured as far into the realm of the spectacular. According to a press release from the producers of this work (which, granted, may be exaggerated), the scene showing the collapse of the trestle with the train cost forty thousand dollars. An expensive gag—probably the highest ever paid for one joke. Today such a scene in a comedy would probably be done with miniatures, but this was the fabulous Twenties when the competition between high-ranking comedians ran high, and new and better thrills were needed. Keaton, it would seem, was taking his cue from Harold Lloyd in the creation of "thrill" comedy. Keaton's working method for plotting his films paralleled Lloyd's—he did not handle his material the way Chaplin and Langdon developed their plots. He is quoted by John Montgomery as saying:

> The best way to get a laugh is to create a genuine thrill and then relieve the tension with comedy. Getting laughs depends on the element of surprise, and surprises are harder and harder to get as audiences, seeing more pictures, become more and more comedy-wise.[19]

But Keaton didn't resort to steeplejacking thrills as Chaplin did when he seemed to be imitating Lloyd's use of such material.

Johnny Gray in *The General* displays a character similar to the young man in *Sherlock, Jr.* and does not have the characteristics of the blasé Rollo Treadway of *The Navigator*. Johnny's obsession with his locomotive is as strong as the obsession of the amateur detective. This character also has some of the facets of the personalities of the genteel comedy. He is, after all, a small town boy trying to make good in a hostile world. In this aspect, Keaton also seems to be taking his cue from Harold Lloyd.

I believe that the comic character's relationship with his girl, which is most pronounced in *The General*, helps to distinguish his comic protagonist from the other comedians' clowns. Both Chaplin's and Lloyd's comic characters are intensely interested in young women. Even Langdon's child-like little fellow yearns for a girl. Keaton's comic personality seems to have a girl because "it's the thing to do." As the *Motion Picture Magazine's* reviewer observes, Keaton develops a type of dumb heroine that is a fresh concept in the comic film.[60] Chaplin, Lloyd, and Langdon employed the sweet, innocent type of female in their films. Keaton pioneers in this use of female characterisation for comedy. Furthermore, Keaton has his comic character Johnny, in *The General*, treat his girl as if she were an unwanted sister who was just along "for the ride."

In all the features examined in this chapter (including *Our Hospitality*, a work that has been discussed only briefly), Keaton's comic character has been shown to be created on a realistic basis and to be integral with the plot development. Those critics who try to apply Henri Bergson's comic theory of mechanism to his character are only looking at that facet which appeals to them. True, Keaton achieves some of his best comedy by the machine-like workings of his comic character, but the exclusion of other facets of his portrayal (especially its link with the genteel comedy character) seems to be a grievous simplification of Keaton's comedy. Such analyses are clever but not as original or profound as these evaluators would like the reader to believe.

Furthermore, after an intensive examination of his features, one can conclude that Keaton's character is both an asset and a liability. While many critics see the uniqueness of the role the comedian plays, they do not seem to see its limitations. The character promotes laughter best when the deluge comes, when an army pursues. Regardless of the maelstrom or mayhem that engulfs this character, his anaesthetised face muscles barely flicker even though his body may be bent at a forty-five degree angle against chaos. The character's nearly zero reaction is the root of Keaton's clown; and such a reaction restricts the variety of gags that can be created without being inconsistent. Furthermore, this limitation of reaction does not allow the dimension which both Lloyd and Chaplin have in their characters. The audience may find enough normal reactions to sympathise with the plight of their clowns. Keaton cannot make an audience so involved with the fate of his simpleton; and such audience interest is necessary in the building of a dramatic story. It was a problem of comedy creation that was built into the clown that Harry Langdon employed—his character, as it will be shown in the next chapter, had a similar limitation.

Both Keaton and Lloyd have developed comic films that will not age with the passing of time. The timelessness of their films is based on the universals that they express with their comic characters coupled with the anti-sentimental approach to their material. While some of the plot material and the characterisational types are borrowed from the genteel comedy, both of these men are able to twist the sentimental moments into a good gag. At the end of his films, Keaton (like Lloyd) often ties up the resolution with a sharp laugh at the tender, tear evoking moment. As the amateur sleuth in *Sherlock, Jr.* is about to embrace his loved one in the projection booth of a theatre, he finds that he must take instruction from the movie being shown in order to carry out his amorous activities. In *The General* Johnny Gray is commissioned as an officer in the Confederate army and finds that when a line of enlisted men pass him, he must interrupt his embraces with Annabelle to salute. He solves the dilemma by performing both actions at the same time.

6. A Little Boy in a Big World

HE HAD THE stamp of Pierrot and the tight smile of an idiot child. Pathetic in his loneliness, his character was a charming little fellow. With a rare gift for subtle, smooth pantomime, Harry Langdon rose from a mediocre position as a vaudeville comedian in a skit called "Johnny's New Car" to rival and nearly equal the great clowns who already had achieved success in the motion pictures. For two years, 1926 and 1927, he was the rage of the Hollywood community and the darling of the New York critics. But this star plunged into the obscure, desolate plains of second-rate films more quickly than he ascended. His brilliance faded to a faint glow among the refuse of the might-have-beens and the has-beens. He was a gag writer and a sometime actor in the Thirties and Forties; he died in 1944, remembered by the few. A legacy of his films from the years 1924 to 1927 verify Langdon's greatness—his inventiveness and his individuality.

Few historians and critics of the movies have given Langdon the high rank he deserves. While James Agee rated him higher than most commentators, he described the comedian as a "virtuoso of hesitation and of delicately indecisive motions" and observed that he had "a subtle emotional and mental process" similar to Chaplin's.[27] Agee, like others, was most flattering when he attributed characteristics of Langdon's acting to his alleged imitation of other comedians. Bardèche and Brasillach called him a "student" of Chaplin, and a *New York Times* critic of his *Long Pants* (1927) wrote: "Mr. Langdon is still Charles Spenser Chaplin's sincerest flatterer. His short coat reminds one of Chaplin and now and again his foot work is like that of the great screen comedian."[67] Other evaluators of the times compared him to Larry Semon and even saw, in his half-hearted gestures, similarities to the acting style of comedienne Zasu Pitts.*

While such observations have merit and some validity, I believe they are oversimplifications. From a detailed study of Langdon's films, one can note unique characteristics—characteristics that used a comic style and comic material tailored to his particular talents. Langdon's unique features made him a great comedian.

The most obvious difference between Langdon's and Chaplin's characters is in mentality. Langdon falls into the class of "dumb" clowns. Most of the humour of his character springs from a child-like man who is lost in a sophisticated world.

*Especially illuminating material on such comparisons may be found in the Museum of Modern Art Film Library in *Weinberg Scrapbooks of Film Reviews*, Volume I, 1925–1927.

Unlike Chaplin's character, this little fellow is a simpleton who seldom takes action; he is a sexless baby who concentrates on his bag of popcorn when a woman of ill-repute makes eyes at him. Without a will of any consequence, this frail creature evokes laughter and sympathy when he is pitted against physical and mental superiors. We chuckle at his intense curiosity as he examines objects such as machines, buildings, and landscapes; or, animals, a very fat woman, or the beard of a dignified gentleman, with all the wide-eyed wonder of a four year old. This is certainly not Chaplin's character. Langdon's image is closer to the type of clown created by Stan Laurel. In fact, some awareness of the similarities led to an unsuccessful attempt to pair Langdon with Oliver Hardy in *Zenobia* (1939).[18]

But Langdon's character did not crystallise when he first entered motion pictures. His early one- and two-reel works for Mack Sennett showed little promise. A very good example of weak and inconsistent character development was displayed in *Picking Peaches* (1924). Misleading characteristics appear in the beginning episode of the film when Harry portrays a shy, fumbling, and dim-witted clerk in a shoe store; immediately following this portion, he is shown stepping out with a woman, in a beach sequence that is replete with Sennett's bathing beauties. While Langdon attempts to give his character the qualities of a child-like lover, inconsistency sets in when the script calls for him to be a "lady killer." Despite such conceptual weakness in the drawing of his character (the writers and director are mostly to blame, it would seem), Langdon's acting is especially effective when he is discovered in a boudoir by a suspicious husband. His face flickers with child-like terror as he hides under the bed covers, only to have the husband get into bed with him—believing that Harry is his wife. It is a beautifully executed moment—a moment that forecast more to come from this comedian.

With Frank Capra and Arthur Ripley writing for his *Lucky Star* (1925), considerable growth in story line and character development was displayed. The plot was simple, direct, and less contrived than the usual product ground out by the Sennett comedy mill. Most of the comic incidents are rooted in character. Plot material may have been gleaned from Langdon's experiences as a boy because the whole action centres around the hapless comic character's struggles as an assistant to the medicine man of a travelling show.* Langdon's character is shown pitted against the charms of a *femme fatale*—story material that was more completely exploited in his feature films.

As he neared the time that he was to skyrocket to popularity in 1925, Langdon's character began to come into focus. His comic forte—the confused hesitations and eventual rejection of a laboured impulse were turned to perfection; and his childlike obsession with either ordinary or unusual features of objects, animals, or humans was being masterfully handled in pantomime. For example, Harry is shown reacting to a bearded lady in a circus in *Remember When?*, a film of 1925 vintage. The dilemma of the little fellow is artfully mimed as Harry strains his feeble brain trying to decide whether he should take off his hat or shake hands. Then he hesitates for a moment and thinks about giving the bearded lady a cigar but rejects the idea. His unquenchable curiosity prompts him to touch her beard and

*Langdon reported that he got seven dollars a week working with Dr. Staley's medicine show. (From an interview by Madeline Matzen[39]).

then touch his own face (that can only be said to have a beard the consistency of peach fuzz) and, somewhat satisfied, he smiles weakly and coyly at the woman before him.

On the eve of his entrance into features, Langdon's direction was further solidified by *Soldier Man*, a film copyrighted April 28, 1926.* While it was not the practice to review short films at this time, the *National Board of Review Magazine* found enough merit in Langdon's war comedy in its May–June issue to declare telegraphically, "Slapstick but some real humour." Interest in this three-reel work may have developed because of the elaborate production and characteristics that were very much like those of a feature work. Eight sequences are needed to tell the story of a World War I soldier who doubles for a king of a foreign country. The sets are varied and elaborate for such a short work; the cast is much larger than usual. But the quality of the film lies in Harry Langdon's gift for comic pantomime.

Since the first half of the story depends a great deal on the comedian's portrayal, some of the most interesting comic incidents are developed in this portion of the film. His "little boy lost" character is fully exploited as he is shown wandering over the battlefields after peace has been declared. The heroic pose is mocked when the little fellow mistakes the dynamiting of three stumps for enemy artillery. A close-up of Harry's written declaration in his "war diary" reveals the much-ado-about-nothing nature of the humour in this situation: "The artillery has located me. Will try to hold this post to the finish." Harry locates and pursues a "Bomanian" farmer, believing him

*In the year of 1926 the comedian was highly prolific. His first feature length comedy *Tramp, Tramp, Tramp* was released in May, and his highly successful *The Strong Man* received rave reviews in September.

to be the enemy. In the course of this chase, Harry lies on his stomach under a milk cow. Langdon exhibits one of the most unique, clever comic touches of the picture—a comic touch so ingrained in the specific comic character that it easily illustrates his difference from other comedians. A scenario that I have prepared from the film shows clearly the skill of the mime and the clever editing of the incident:

> 91 MLS Harry lies on his stomach with the udders of the cow in left frame (Harry's right). He looks forward blankly, not noticing the cow's "special equipment." Slightly shifting his head, he discovers the phenomenon. He stares at the udders, blinks and looks forward again; but his fascination with the four objects hanging near his face draws his gaze back. In blank puzzlement he brings his hand up and touches one of the tits lightly. It swings before him. Again he touches this front udder. A childish grin comes over his face as he taps the tit once more absentmindedly and looks front. He drops his hand and stares at the objects again.
>
> 92 CU The cow turns her head toward frame left as if looking backwards and down at Harry, who is off frame left.
>
> 93 MLS (same angle as shot 91) Harry looks off frame right at the cow, whose head is not visible. There is a slight grin on his face. He is once more drawn back by the sight of the udders. . . .

Much of *Soldier Man*'s weakness lies in its disunity—a fault that plagues an otherwise skilfully conceived work, *The Strong Man*. The comic potentials of Langdon as a boy-man playing soldier are abruptly dismissed when the comic character is forced to substitute for the true monarch, "King Strudel the

Thirteenth," a double in appearance who has been kidnapped. Intrigue of this sort doesn't seem to assist Langdon's comic abilities, but there are moments when the film sparkles as Harry tries ineptly to play the role of a king. In the climactic sequence of the film, the comedy that best suited Langdon's abilities reigns. Pitted against a *femme fatale* again, the Queen of Bomania, the comic protagonist becomes more concerned with food than with the advances of a beautiful woman. Nevertheless, after her insistent requests, he administers reluctant kisses that melt the desire of the woman to kill him. The Queen of Bomania faints from the unseen charm of the stoic little lover. The film's resolution has the same contrived feature as Chaplin's 1918 comic thesis on life in the trenches, *Shoulder Arms*. The intrigue that makes up the body of the film is discovered to be all a dream.

When Langdon released his first full-length screen comedy, *Tramp, Tramp, Tramp*, the fan magazine *Photoplay* greeted his work with this statement:

> This picture takes Harry Langdon's doleful face and pathetic figure out of the two-reel class and into the Chaplin and Lloyd screen dimensions. Not that he equals their standing yet, but he is a worthy addition to a group of comedy makers of which we have entirely too few. Langdon has graduated and this picture is his diploma.[69]

And Laurence Reid wrote a rave review of the film, pointing out Langdon's unique comedy that he believed generated laughs "without resorting to imitations of other comedians' gags."[61] This view may be stated because of Langdon's character and not because of his material. He used "thrill comedy" (which had been thoroughly exploited by Harold

Lloyd) by showing his comic character caught on a fence and dangling over a cliff.* His attempt to win a race (a transcontinental hiking contest) in order to win the girl seems like derivative material from the genteel comedians Charles Ray, Douglas MacLean, and Johnnie Hines. Nevertheless, the battery of gag writers, with Frank Capra in the foreground and director Harry Edwards, tailored the material for the special talents of their star comedian.

The shifting of personnel in his production staff seemed to secure the comedian's fortune and future. With Frank Capra as director and Arthur Ripley as writer, Langdon took the final, giant step up the ladder of popular and critical acclaim. New York critics such as Richard Watts, Jr. were rhapsodic in their praise of his work in *The Strong Man*, a film released in September 1926.

In their admiration of the comedian's genius for character development and mime, many critics seemed to overlook structural weaknesses. The story line of the total film is divided into the war activities of the comic hero, his search in the big city for a girl he knows only through correspondence, and his discovery of the girl in a small town, and his defeat of corrupt forces in the town. The mild little man's search is too desultory —too erratic and mis-directed to provide a plot line of any strength. Such a weakness seems inherent in the leading comedian's character. The comic portrait of most leading silent screen comedians, with the exception of Harold Lloyd's, is woefully lacking in will. The power to take action is nearly nil in such lost souls, and only on rare occasions do such characters

*Langdon claimed that without a stunt man he executed this dangerous incident over a cliff of "several hundred yards with nothing to break the fall."[37]

fight their adversaries or succeed in eliminating an obstacle in their paths. Since comic weakness and dumbness is so great a facet of Langdon's character, his works are apt to be plagued with weak plot lines.

While *The Strong Man* is an episodic work, there are many scenes which attest to Langdon's comic genius and account for his popular and critical acclaim in the late 1920's. An outstanding comic sequence can be observed in the portion of the film which shows the meek little protagonist being used as a front by a gangster's moll, Lily. After she has slipped a money roll into Harry's coat pocket, this hard-faced woman announces that she is Mary Brown, the girl he is seeking. As Harry courts the bogus Mary Brown with a bag of popcorn and a joyful yet sheepish smile, Lily tries to regain the money that she has concealed in his pocket. Langdon's best and most unique comic scenes in the film develop from this situation. One of the best examples is as follows:

> 298 LMS Inside a moving cab, Harry (left) and Lily (right) are seated facing the camera. He smilingly puts a grain of popcorn in his mouth. She puts her hand under his chin affectionately. He looks at her hand vaguely and she withdraws. He touches his own chin; then, pats her chin weakly in childlike imitation. Harry pats her hands vaguely and eats his popcorn gleefully. He looks out the window of the cab—almost standing up. She seizes the opportunity and feels the roll of money in his coat pocket. (The roll has slipped from a hole in the lining of the pocket and is now shifted to the rear of his coat.) Harry sits down again and points out the sights to her. He offers her some popcorn; she refuses. Lily puts her arm around his neck and pats his shoulder.

THE GENERAL (1927). Top: as Johnny Gray, Keaton shows his acrobatic skills by picking up obstacles in front of his locomotive and is pushed off balance as the slowly moving engine catches up with him. Below: a posed shot that does not appear in the final print but one that reveals a basic facet of the character Keaton created.

*eft: Harry Lang-
on in the 1927
ONG PANTS—
he hapless child-
tan is caught be-
veen two women.
ight: two frame
nlargements from
OLDIER MAN
1926) — at top,
'arry looking for
is regiment and,
elow, the child-man
iscinated by the
dders of a cow.*

THE STRONG MAN (1926).
Top: the little fellow faces an angry mob
Below: an effete punch is aimed at an annoyed fellow traveller.

He playfully tries to put popcorn into her mouth. Her arm drops out of sight. Suddenly Harry's face falls in amazement; his feet come forward and he slides down with popcorn flying. He looks at her with a puzzled (almost horrified) expression and slowly puts a kernel of popcorn into his mouth. Lily feigns innocence and lights a cigarette. Harry moves into the corner of the cab with a frightened, amazed expression on his pale face. He pulls a photo out of his pocket and looks down at it.

299 CU The photo of Mary Brown.

300 LMS Harry pockets the photo and gets up as if to leave the moving cab. She pulls him back; he holds on to his hat and cowers in the corner. Lily puts her arm around him, playfully unbuttoning his coat. He twitches in horror—popcorn flying; he pulls his coat quickly around himself. At the same time he holds onto his hat. He tries to get out of the cab, and she grabs him to prevent him from jumping.

Shortly after this scene, director Capra and writer Ripley continue to exploit such material. Harry is cornered in the woman's apartment. While she seeks the money, the child-man believes his virtue is at stake. He scrambles over furniture and pulls a good portion of the tapestry from the walls in his flight. The scene becomes an unusual comic inversion that burlesques the stock "rape" scene of the 1920's movie, when an innocent girl from the country is pursued by a lust-filled city slicker.

After Harry weakly submits to a kiss from the *femme fatale* (and consequently is deprived of the money he does not know is in his suit coat), a clever title by Ripley tops the scene. Harry meekly goes to the door, crushed by what he thinks is a loss of his virtue. A title flashed on the screen shows verbal humour supporting Harry's painful facial expression: "Don't let this leak out!" He gestures vaguely, opens the door, and hides his face as he passes a woman in the hallway. This sequence (the third in the film) shows the unique province of Harry Langdon—no other major comedian of the Twenties exploited the comic character's fear of being seduced sexually.

Another outstanding sequence in *The Strong Man* proves to be the most tangential portion of the film. Organically the episode serves no function. It does not further the plot or develop the comic portrait of the leading character. Nevertheless, it is very funny. It is a portion of the film (sequence five) which was unanimously lauded by the critics. And, while I object to the unskilful placement and unmotivated nature of this episode, I believe it is one of Langdon's best. His skill in creating a great deal of humour from very slight, seemingly insignificant material, illustrates the comedian's pantomimic genius.

The sequence opens with Harry in the front seat of a bus—his back against a partition that separates the driver from the occupants. Thus, Harry faces all the other passengers in the vehicle. Much to everyone's annoyance Harry sniffs, coughs, and sneezes. A dapper young man with a moustache ridicules him vehemently: "Say, what did you swallow—a fish horn?" and "If you feel like you sound, you need a plumber." The wisecracking enemy glares at the little man's ritual of forcing himself to take cough syrup. Harry holds an argument with himself —shrinking at the thought of the medicine's taste. Just as he decides to brave the bitterness of the black liquid, he sneezes and spatters syrup over the dapper foe. Angrily the man wipes the medicine from his face and clothes, viciously declaring, "One more germ out of you and Smith Brothers will lose a good customer!"

Langdon then executes one of the best moments of the film:

> 529 MS Harry (facing camera) looks at the gentleman from the extreme corners of his eyes. It is a sharp, childlike glare.
> 530 LMS Harry (left frame) glares with extreme concentration. The man (right frame) reads his paper, ignoring Harry. Without warning the little fellow jabs with a short, weak punch to the gentleman's jaw. With obvious skill, the man relatiates with a sharp, hard punch that sends Harry flying back against the partition. Even though startled, Harry frantically grabs his hat to prevent it from falling.

Some of Langdon's best pantomime in the film is evidenced by such clever handling of the situations in this eleven-minute sequence.

Langdon also develops pantomimic material that has some similarity to that employed by Charles Chaplin. When his little clown meets the blind Mary Brown for the first time, he tries to develop sympathy for the little man in a somewhat Chaplinesque fashion. Not realising that Mary is blind, Harry struts before her like a bantam rooster and alternates this pose with shy glances. "Are you surprised to see me?" he asks. Slowly it dawns on him that Mary is blind. He looks at her with sadness and great concern. Then, he proceeds to woo her as if nothing were wrong.

By the use of such material, Langdon (under the guidance of Frank Capra) was able to give dimension to his clown. While the situations are similar to those used by Chaplin, the difference in the comedians' characters provides contrasting treatments. Langdon cannot be accused of blatantly imitating Chaplin as some critics have suggested. In fact, a case could be developed for the view that Chaplin imitated his rivals. The use of the blind heroine by Langdon in the 1926 feature, *The Strong Man*, seems to be the precursor to the use of the same type of character in Chaplin's *City Lights* in 1931. Chaplin used climactic "thrill" sequences showing the little tramp at dangerous heights in *The Gold Rush* (1926) and *The Circus* (1928)—material that was developed by Lloyd in the same portion of the film *Safety Last* (1923) and in his earlier one- and two-reel works.

It should be clear that all comedians of the silent screen had traditional comic material at their fingertips and that they used it as common property. They also borrowed and elaborated on material which had proved successful in current comic and serious films. Their individual treatment and specifically different comic characters, of course, cast the material into another key—often providing original twists on familiar situations that prevented the cry of "old hat" from the critics and their audiences.

Langdon, under the guidance of Capra, employed the melodramatic, thrilling climax in *The Strong Man* and thereby followed the pattern and practice firmly established by Lloyd and Keaton at this time. Such a sequence does not add a great deal to Langdon's repertoire of grimaces and nimble footwork, but it does provide a strong, increasingly clever series of gags to round out the picture. In this episode Harry defends Mary Brown's good name by pitting himself against a whole tavern full of angry men. With comic ingenuity he bombards the crowd with bottles as he swings over their heads on a trapeze. He turns back this tide of bullies with a circus cannon filled with various weight-lifting devices. By these unusual feats he unconsciously becomes a reformer and a hero to the people of the vice-ridden town of Cloverdale.

While Langdon's last successful feature, *Long Pants* (1927), adds little that is new to the comedian's comic portrait, the total work displays a tighter plot with few of the diversions that adversely affect the unity of *The Strong Man*. In eight sequences Ripley and Capra have fashioned a story which best employs the character of the little boy in a big world. Harry is shown as the small town child-man in the sophisticated environment of the big city. Interestingly enough, the little fellow does not succeed in the big city as Harold Lloyd's young man striving upward does. He comes home to the girl he left behind in a charming final scene which has all the earmarks of Frank Capra's use of sentiment at its best. Of this work the *National Board of Review Magazine* writes:

> The picture is replete with hilarious gags which give the comedian many opportunities of displaying his woe-begone humour. He is particularly funny when he sets out to shoot his bride with an old horse pistol after the pattern of the unscrupulous villains of whom he has been reading, as well as in the scene where he seeks to impress the adventuress with his skill as a bicycle rider.[64]

Langdon also shows considerable pantomimic ability when he tries to attract the attention of a stage prop dummy policeman. He makes a series of overtures to move the inanimate object into following him. Each gesture becomes more desperate until the poor, dimwitted little fellow is feigning a stroke on the sidewalk. When it finally dawns on him that he may have been wasting his time, a stage hand removes the mannequin and a real policeman takes its place at the stage door. Disgusted with all his wasted efforts, Harry takes a brick and hits the real cop on the head—and, of course, finally has a policeman running after him. While this re-telling of the situation seems to indicate contrived material, Langdon's execution of the routine makes the scene plausible and very laughable.

More than any other work by Langdon, *Long Pants* shows the influence of the genteel comedy. His pursuit of the adventuress is prompted by a misunderstanding. He discovers her note to her boy-friend and assumes that he has captured her affections. This note spurs Harry to get rid of his small town girl friend and journey to the big city. When he seeks the adventuress there, the conflict that was often used by Charles Ray and Harold Lloyd is obvious. Harry is the country boy against the city slickers.

Frank Capra's hand is also more evident in *Long Pants*. It can be rated as Langdon's best picture if the film is viewed as a total work. Capra's control of the story, the camera, and his actors makes it one of the best silent screen comedies. *Long Pants* was made at the height of Langdon's career. Unfortunately the comedian was not satisfied with Capra as a director and dismissed him from his company. It was a fateful decision that spelled the rapid fall of Langdon's career. While Chaplin, Lloyd, and Keaton furthered their best efforts by taking firm control of their films, Langdon suffered greatly. Evidently he was not the judge of his comic skills that Frank Capra had been.

Theory-wise, Langdon wrote about the nature of comedy with some insight. He recognised the value of an effective characterisation, good gag writers, and many of the skills needed to execute a comic routine. At the height of his fame, however, he became too obsessed with the serious elements which were often the counterpoint, the added flavour and dimension of his and Chaplin's films. He produced this over-simplified, somewhat garbled view on the eve of his fall:

> Comedy is the satire of tragedy. Serious matters repeated turn to comic as they pass through a morbidly active conscience. Most deliciously comic moments on the outside, are full of sad significances for those who realize the sinister characterisation of the situation.[37]

With Langdon supervising the ill-fated *Three's a Crowd* (1927), the use of what some writers have called "Chaplinesque pathos" backfired. The fan magazines and the New York critics who had found their darling turned full circle were disenchanted and fired devastating volleys of criticism at this work. One fan magazine, for example, wrote:

> Harry Langdon reaches for the moon in this and grasps—a feeble glow-worm. He has tried to stuff the plots of Chaplin's "The Kid" and Charlie Ray's "The Girl I Loved" into one picture. The result is an absurd, unbelievable story. To top the blunder he makes you wade through thick layers of oleomargarine pathos to get at the comedy. Harry clowns the part of a trunk heaver who always has wanted a wife and a child. It didn't matter whose they were. He gets his wish one day but they are reclaimed. We like Harry Langdon and hate to hear the sound of his flops. May his next be louder and funnier.[68]

But the comedian didn't become "louder and funnier." He never recovered from this failure.

While I find most of Langdon's features and many of his short films very funny, the whimsy of his comic portrait has not been widely accepted. Most audiences and critics of today that have been fortunate enough to see some of his films recognise the sublety of his acting and acknowledge an elusive, undefinable charm in his comedy. But, the naivety of his comic character limits his appeal. Langdon was prevented from executing the variety of gags that Chaplin and Lloyd could handle because of their complex characterisations. He seems to wear thin with some people in a very short time.

The faults of Langdon's work, therefore, place him lower on the comic achievement scale than Chaplin and Lloyd. Lack of will in the character limits story development. Seldom did little Harry take action against his sea of troubles. Both Chaplin's and Lloyd's characters had an aggressive facet in their personalities and thus got involved in sharp, strong struggles. They had moments of violent action—kicking and biting their opposition—generally a bully twice their size. Their works were sprinkled with the spice of invective comedy which provided variety and helped move the story along with a vital, fast-paced conflict. Comic invention sometimes lagged in Langdon's works. Seldom was there a scene approaching the dizzily moving sequences of Lloyd's works. Detailed pantomimed routines were his forte—but Chaplin could execute such comic "bits" more effectively.

My attraction to Langdon's comedy is seated in his acting. Like Chaplin in his approach to his little tramp, Langdon brought an intensity to his portrayal of his little-boy-lost that is captivating. Langdon seemed to live the role he was acting. In fact, critics of the Twenties had difficulty separating the comic character and the man, Langdon. Some writers for the fan magazines reported that he was much like his screen character in real life, and others wrote that he was a clever, intelligent artist. The former is unlikely—a boob cannot play a boob; the latter view, though exaggerated, is closer to the truth. Langdon needed a director who understood his type of comedy, but he was the skilled creator of an unusual comic character. After all, he had been successful in vaudeville with skits which he created for himself; he was also a talented cartoonist.

With all his faults, Langdon's virtues are strong enough for a king's robe. And, I believe, he will remain in the king's row with Chaplin, Lloyd, and Keaton, as long as his films are preserved for posterity.

7. The Perfection of the Feature Comedy

"IT WENT farther than the park comedy," Harold Lloyd explained. I agreed with Lloyd and remarked that I had examined his first film comedy, *Just Nuts* (1915), at the Museum of Modern Art Film Library only a year previous to our interviews.* *Just Nuts* tried to break away from the formula: "mo" clothes on the "lead", a beautiful girl, and a "heavy" in a policeman's uniform. With these ingredients inciting them, the early film-makers packed a camera, drove to the park and began their impromptu shooting of a vaguely conceived comic plot. Three of the top comedians of the Twenties, Chaplin, Lloyd, and Keaton, went through a formative period in the 1910's with a simple, utilitarian, inexpensive approach similar to this primitive formula. By the middle Twenties they had evolved an elaborate, carefully planned approach, integrating some of the

*The interviews with Harold Lloyd (and Buster Keaton) in this chapter were obtained by visits in Beverly Hills and Hollywood and telephone conversations in June 1965.

flexibility of the impromptu "park method" of creating a comedy film.

I feel that Lloyd and Keaton were largely responsible for developing the feature comedy into an effective, vital genre. Chaplin, of course, had his foot in the door earlier with *The Kid* in 1921, and Sennett pioneered with *Tillie's Punctured Romance* as early as 1915. But I believe Lloyd and Keaton to be major perfectors of the feature comedy. They were successful in developing this genre because of their concern with the main comic character, the story line and structure, appropriate gags, and finally, the judicious use of "sneak previews."

Both Lloyd and Keaton obtained a control of their total works that allowed them leeway to perfect the comedy film. And, of course, Chaplin who was, more than these two, the sole creator, made a substantial contribution to the development of the comedy feature. Because he was not as productive during the Twenties and remained relatively silent about his working methods, Chaplin did not seem to play the same role of perfector as did Lloyd and Keaton.

When I asked Buster Keaton in 1965 his opinion of Harold Lloyd's work, he replied that he found him a "great picture man —an experimenter." Keaton's statement indicated his admiration for Lloyd's workmanship—his ability to construct novel comedy films. From all indications, Lloyd has also admired Keaton's ability to spin an excellent comic tale, for he told me that he was appalled by the cut, mutilated, and condensed version of Keaton's *The General* on the television series "Silents Please." Lloyd declined to narrate this series because he respected the artistry of his contemporaries and imagined how he would feel if someone handled his work in a similar way. While Lloyd has allowed sequences of his films to be presented in his *Harold Lloyd's World of Comedy*, he has resisted attempts by well-meaning production personnel to condense his works or alter a total work by cutting. He indicated to me that any cutting which he plans for future releases of his silent screen works will be of a minor nature. I witnessed the product of his editing technique when Lloyd graciously presented a preview of his *Harold Lloyd's Funny Side of Life*—a film that features the total work, *The Freshman*, with some special sequences from *For Heaven's Sake* (1926), *The Kid Brother* (1927), and *Speedy* (1928). In the complete work, Lloyd had deleted a few minor scenes, such as a topical gag on radio hams which would be meaningful to very few people in an audience under forty years of age.

The concentrated attention paid to the overall structure of their films was an essential part of the working methods of Lloyd and Keaton. In 1924 in both of their contributions to Laurence Hughes's *The Truth About the Movies*, they displayed a sense of historical development of the comic film and concentrated their discussions on the need for well-motivated situations, gags, and effective story construction. Interestingly enough, Chaplin submitted a slight, fan magazine type of article on becoming a star in this same book.

In my interviews with Lloyd and Keaton, I found these comedians still as concerned about the basic problems of comedy film making today as they were in 1924. Their works show that both were most anxious to create the best stories for their characters. Keaton wrote in his autobiography that "the story was always the thing, with the star next in performance."[14] Lloyd told me, as he told Arthur Friedman,[33] that he concentrated first on a theme from which he evolved a story—a story that was carefully worked and reworked during the shooting.

This insistence on a clear-cut, logical story line made the two comedians the producers of some of the tightest, strongest comedies of the Twenties. Coupled with this concern was the very careful construction of situations and individual gags.

Keaton told me that one of his most difficult structural problems resulted from the misplaced gag. He explained that he often needed to throw out a gag because it did not fit his character or the story, that such discarded gags might be employed in another portion of the same film or used in another picture. He also expressed this concern with writing by mentioning that he had to cut a gag in *The Navigator* which showed him in a deep sea diving outfit, directing the fish traffic on the bottom of the ocean, because it interfered with the progression of the story line.

Lloyd's autobiography, like Keaton's, displays his concentration on the dangers of the misplaced or inappropriate gag. He pointed out the working method of creating more gags in story conferences than could be used in the film. Of these gags he wrote: "Some we discard without trial, others will be edited out."[17] Furthermore, Lloyd revealed to me that he generally tried to avoid a "fantastic gag"—one where the laugh was gained by the impossible nature of the situation—the type most often seen in animated cartoons. He admitted that he yielded to temptation by using this type in *Get Out and Get Under* (1920) when his comic protagonist tried to fix a recalcitrant car. He showed his character climbing farther and farther under the hood of the engine until he disappeared. An arm reaching up for tools accentuated the absurdity of his position inside the car where the presence of the motor would obviously not allow his whole body to fit. Lloyd claims this incident was one of the few times he departed from and defied logic to get a laugh.

Keaton has also indicated that he used the fantastic gag in such two-reelers as *Hard Luck* (1921) where he missed a dive into a swimming pool and went crashing into an adjoining cement walk. "Years later," as the title indicated, a new scene showed him climbing out of the hole dressed in a Chinese costume and followed by a Chinese wife and children. To Keaton such a gag was fit only for cartoons or his two-reel works; he considered them out of place in a feature film. In his major five- to eight-reel works he felt that he needed to concentrate on credible material in order to sustain the film—to keep the audience tied up in the story and the comic character. Fantastic gags, he believed, were a detriment to this method of creating a feature that would hold an audience over a long period of time.[14] The sequence I described in the fifth chapter which portrays the comedian as a victim of editing when he enters the movie screen projection during the first part of an elaborate dream (the core of the film) may seem to contain gags of this nature. This portion of *Sherlock, Jr.*, however, cannot be classified as an extended use of the fantastic gag. There is dream logic in this unique humorous episode. Keaton himself saw this use of the medium as a logical development. He seemed proud of this portion not only because the critics found it so intriguing but also because of the fact that many cameramen of that time (1924) went to the picture to figure out what they thought was trick photography. As Keaton explained to Christopher Bishop, sets with a construction that gave the appearance of a motion picture frame were built for each shot; with the changing of each scene minute measurements had to be made to make sure Keaton and the camera were placed in the same location they had occupied in the previous scene.[28]

Probably one of the most difficult things to determine is the originality of a gag used by a comedian. It is often a pointless pursuit because gags are common property that can be altered to fit a particular motion picture story. For instance, Jacques Tati's perplexed comic character in the present day *Mr. Hulot's Holiday* tries to interpret a series of arm movements protruding from a car ahead of him—not knowing whether the vehicle means to turn left or right or stop. The arms, in this case, belong to excited sightseers who are sharing the scenery with their companions. In Lloyd's 1920 two-reeler, *Haunted Spooks*, the "signals" are produced by two old Jewish men holding a conversation as they drive down the street. Tati, it would seem, has refurbished this joke by working it into his film to fit the situation and his comic character.

With gags as common property comedians have playfully (and sometimes scornfully) accused each other of lifting a gag when the latest products hit the movie market. Both Lloyd and Keaton admitted that some problem of originality has always plagued them to a degree and that much of what we identify as originality actually lies in the inventive adaptation of the gag to their own style, character, and story. This type of invention was also a working method employed by Chaplin. While there is little indication of this in his writings, it is well known in the world of early film-makers that Chaplin viewed the works of his contemporaries carefully and learned much from them—as they learned from him. There was, in short, a kind of cross-fertilisation of gags, ideas on comic character and situations, and production techniques that made this a great age of comedy.

In the handling of their comic material, it is clear that Lloyd and Keaton demanded a firm control on the complete creative process. They possessed not only the acting skill to create superior comic works; they also had a taste in comedy superior to that of most of their gag writers and other production personnel. Both men told me that when they had such control they did their best work. It can also be said that when they were forced by production techniques and the studio hierarchy (especially in the Thirties) to compromise that control and taste for comedy, their works suffered. In his autobiography Keaton complains of well-meaning attempts, such as the attempt of the studio bosses to insist on the use of a written scenario for *The Cameraman.*[14] In an interview with Christopher Bishop he tells of co-director Donald Crisp's effort to be a gag man for *The Navigator* even though he was specifically hired to direct the action and serious scenes of the film.[28] He also tells in his autobiography of a staff of twenty-two writers for *The Cameraman* who were contributing mountains of material so that a simple plot became complicated with "gangsters, Salvation Army street bands, Tammany Hall politicians, longshoremen, and lady gem thieves." He further complains that it wasn't only the writers who were eager to help—"the executives and studio big shots also turned into gagmen overnight, adding greatly to the confusion. With so much talk going on, so many conferences, so many brains at work, I began to lose faith for the first time in my own ideas."[14]

I believe Lloyd must have been victimised to a lesser degree by similar developments. He indicated to me that he had many problems with his last feature, *Mad Wednesday* (1947), because he compromised with Preston Sturges, a director who seemed to think Lloyd's style and his use of material akin to the primitive slapstick of Mack Sennett, vintage 1914. Obviously Lloyd needed a Sam Taylor or a Fred Newmeyer to assist him with such a work—a director who understood his style and his type of material. Taylor, in 1923, indicated his own concern for the story and the proper relationship of the gag to the situation and comic character. He praised Lloyd's comic inventiveness and said that he and the comedian worked together on all phases of the film.[44] The many pictures for which Taylor served as director or co-director were among the best of Lloyd's eighteen features.

Charles Chaplin, it has long been realised, was a comedian who maintained a firm grasp on all phases of his creations. In fact, it is sometimes thought that he may have leaned too heavily on his own judgment—that many of his weaknesses were a result of not listening enough to his advisors and production personnel. In the early Twenties, his secretary, Elsie Codd, observed that a great deal of work was done in story conferences (a practice of all comic film-makers), but also added that Chaplin always reserved the right to cut or add what he thought best for the film.[8] Theodore Huff (as well as many other writers) believed that Chaplin's success lay in the fact that his pictures were a "one man job."[11] This, of course, could be said of Lloyd and Keaton because they had the final word on their films, but I believe these two comedians were more adaptable to valid suggestions. Unlike Chaplin they both gave freely where credit was due to their colleagues and seemed to have a sense of the corporate nature of their creations. But like Chaplin they still demanded control of their works and were given the right in the Twenties to select the best and reject the weaker portions of their films.

Chaplin was probably a sterner taskmaster when it came to advising his actors and production personnel. Mack Swain suggested the influence Chaplin exerted on his cast and crew when he remarked on the change from the early free-wheeling days of the one- and two-reel comedies. "Now at Charlie's studio," he

Other comedians. Top: Snub Pollard almost disappears with his automobile as he hits a rather deep puddle. Below left: Charlie Chase, a comedian with many of the qualities of Harold Lloyd, was never successful in feature length works. Noted for his many two-reelers, he was also a director of other minor comedians under the name of Charles Parrott. Below right: an eccentric comedian, Ben Turpin seemed out of place in sound pictures.

Other comedians. Left: two stills from Laurel and Hardy's LIBERTY (1929)—top the second sequence finds the frustrated pair trying to get the right pants on; and, below the third sequence shows the famous team trying to employ material that Lloyd handled more effectively. Right: W. C. Fields in THE BANK DICK (1940)—he was one of th few silent comedians who made the transition and even became more famous in the sound film

said to an interviewer in 1926, "everything is quiet. There is no talking during a scene and little more between scenes. The cameramen whisper to each other. There is a unity between Charlie and his players."[43] He tells also how he laboured under Chaplin's direction in the starvation sequence of *The Gold Rush*:

> That was the hardest scene in my career, and I've been on the stage and in pictures since I was fifteen. Day after day we would do the same thing over and over. Charlie would say: "Now let's get into it!" Finally I hypnotised myself into a stupor. Food had no taste for me. I would fall asleep in my chair as soon as I came out of the scene. It was a hideous dream—that hypnotic trance. It put me under doctor's care. Then we finished the sequence and went into another part of the picture and I fully recovered.[43]

While Chaplin's working method had many similarities to Lloyd's and Keaton's, the difference seemed to lie in his approach to directing the actors in his films; he appeared to have an iron-fist control over his actors—especially in his works from the Twenties on.

Chaplin has written about his films in a general way, but he has seldom dealt with the specific techniques of his craft. On occasion he has mentioned his method of developing a story, and even more rarely he has written about his use of specific gags. Again it takes an observer, Elsie Codd, to point out that Chaplin determined how to edit his film during the shooting of the picture, that he created brief captions because he felt that the audience didn't want to *read* the story, and that he sometimes used a caption to reinforce a gag that might be unclear to the audience.[8] All these aspects have been discussed freely by Lloyd and Keaton, but Chaplin seldom expressed his own concern about his craftsmanship. And, it should be realised, he had considerable craftsmanship, but evidently thought such matters not important to those who read about his work. As in his recent autobiography, he seemed more concerned with people and events outside his creative efforts. I found one article by Chaplin, "What People Laugh At," in the November 1918 *American Magazine* that comes closer to expressing his practical views on creating a comic film than such complete books as his embarrassingly self-inflating *Charlie Chaplin's Own Story* (1916), the effusive *My Trip Abroad* (1922), and the milder but still disappointing *My Autobiography* (1964). In this brief article in the *American Magazine*, Chaplin tells how he gathered basic material from real life situations, how he tried to work several laughs from one situation, how he diagnosed his films by noting what people laugh at in his pictures; and he gives an accurate analysis of his use of pretension and dignity to gain laughter. As sketchy as this article may be, it nevertheless gives some indication that Chaplin created less instinctively than some writers would lead one to believe. It dispels the inaccurate notion that his natural talents allowed him to create works with very little perspiration.

In a 1967 interview conducted by Richard Meryman,[59] Chaplin gave only a few more clues regarding his craftsmanship. His concern for the exact effect or tone of a scene prompted a number of "takes"—especially for a key scene in *City Lights*:

> I had had several takes and they were all overdone, overacted, overfelt. This time I was looking more at her, interested to see that she didn't make any mistakes. It was a beautiful sensation of not acting, of

standing outside of myself. The key was exactly right—slightly embarrassed, delighted about meeting her again—apologetic without getting emotional about it. He was watching and wondering what she was thinking and wondering without any effort. It's one of the purest inserts—I call them inserts, close-ups—that I've ever done. One of the purest.[59]

While Chaplin skilfully used key close-ups such as this one that has just been described, he was reluctant to use them or other devices of the medium. In this interview he even indicated that he "never liked the close-up too much, except for very important moments of emphasis and intimacy."[59]

As a perfector of the feature length comedy, therefore, Chaplin made no significant contribution in cinematically produced humour—that is, humour created almost exclusively by devices of the medium. He was suspicious of "camera tricks," as he called them, and wanted the camera only to serve as a recorder of the action.

All the major comedians relied a great deal on the "sneak preview" to polish up their final product. This practice was even instituted in the days of the one- and two-reel comedies. Since Chaplin seldom mentioned this technique, I must once more refer to Elsie Codd's observation. She noted that the comedian talked about his use of the unexpectant Los Angeles audience for testing his films as "trying it on the dog."[8]

"Sneak previews", Lloyd informed me, were his equivalent of the Broadway theatre production's method of trying the show on the road to get audience reaction before opening in New York. As in the Broadway show, such tests sometimes resulted in a great deal of "re-writing" before the finished product was placed before its largest and most critical audiences.

I was also amazed to hear that Lloyd sometimes tested his features in the same theatre and immediately following a first-run feature of his strongest competitor, Buster Keaton. On one occasion, Lloyd claimed, his unfinished work, *Safety Last*, did better than a Keaton feature.*

After a preview, Lloyd explained, he did a lot of re-shooting of the elaborate chase sequence in *Grandma's Boy* in order to incorporate more gags in this portion of the picture. Audience reaction indicated to him that more comedy was expected from this sequence. Turning to his autobiography, Lloyd wrote about his attempt during the filming of *The Freshman* to avoid the trite gag of losing his trousers. In the projection room he was warned by his production personnel that he had erred in limiting the "unravelling" sequence to his coat. After three or four previews in the Los Angeles area, Lloyd noted that "the audience demonstrated that it was looking forward eagerly to the pants following the coat, and when they did not, made its disappointment so manifest that, after the lapse of a month, we had to redress the set, call back the cast, including many extras in the ballroom scene, and unravel the trousers."[17] Today Lloyd is still using previews of his works to test the comedy of the Twenties on a general audience. He has received favourable results, which should mean that some of his best features will be released in the near future.

Keaton also wrote about his use of the "sneak preview" and explained that care was taken so that the audience would not know it was being tested—to avoid self-conscious reactions. He told how a variation on the old banana peel gag did not work.

*It is more likely that Lloyd's memory is faulty here. He is probably speaking of one of his later pictures. In 1923 both *The Three Ages* and *Our Hospitality* were released in the fall of the year while *Safety Last* had been released in the spring.

Like Lloyd, he changed a hackneyed joke—the comic fall on a banana peel—around; he shot the scene allowing the comic character to miss the peel. A preview indicated that he had to add a shot in which the character took a pratfall after encountering a second banana peel.[14]

The "sneak preview," therefore, became a highly important phase in the creation of the comic film. It became a working method that provided the comedian with a chance to try out his gags and correct his errors; consequently, the total work was often polished to perfection.

When Harry Langdon broke away from director Frank Capra, he tried to carry the preview method of perfecting a feature one step farther than the other major comedians. In 1927 he tried to let the "sneak preview" audience help him edit *Three's A Crowd.* Earlier practice indicated that previewed films had clearly set patterns of the story line, and only minor editing and retakes were needed after the test with an audience. As Tom Waller explained in *Moving Picture World*, after engaging in this highly experimental previewing-editing method, Langdon's character was given a more predominant part in the first portion of the film instead of "giving away" to other characters, and the serious ending was changed to a comic one.[78] Waller also pointed out that over 200,000 feet of film passed through the editor's hands before a six-reel feature was developed. *Long Pants* (created earlier the same year), on the other hand, had only half this total footage because little re-shooting was necessary under the standard system of editing and previewing.[78] But few conclusions can be drawn from this experiment. Unfortunately, the new method could hardly prove that the audience was right (more likely it could be said to have proved Langdon wrong) because *Three's A Crowd* was a failure.

One more example of the length that comedians of the Twenties went to analyse their audience can be illustrated by a brief examination of P. K. Thomajan's "Lafograph" for Lloyd's *The Kid Brother*. As a "special researcher" for the Harold Lloyd Corporation, Thomajan charted, by the use of an elaborate graph, 138 gags that received strong enough audience reaction to register on an ascending scale that used the terms "titter, chuckle, laugh, outburst, scream, and screech."[75] According to this researcher, "at least a dozen performances were checked and listened in on with pad, pencil and stop watch until an exact evaluation was arrived at for each separate episode." I have taken the information from this graph and transcribed it to show one of the high points of the action after about forty minutes of the film have passed. The comic situation may be understood as it is realised that the comic character, Harold, has brought his girl into his house and has caught his brothers downstairs in their night clothes. They hide just as Harold and Jobyna come in the door. The gag number is listed before the description:

56.	Jobyna asks for water	(Chuckle 3 points up)
57.	Harold sees forms of his brothers	(Laugh 1 point up)
58.	Harold mentions coffee	(Chuckle 2 points up)
59.	Harold and Jobyna enter kitchen; brothers hide	(Laugh 4 points up)
60.	Harold spills pot of coffee	(Laugh 2 points up)
61.	Harold sees trunk and brother behind (it)	(Outburst 1 point up)
62.	Both brothers uncovered and flee outdoors into pouring rain	(Scream 4 points up)

63. View of brothers out in rain (Scream 5 points up)

I know of no other attempts by the creators of comic films of the Twenties to work out such an elaborate design for investigating the effect of their films on an audience. Such a method might seem to some to take away the artistry and intuitive nature of the creation—that such a final product might become mechanical and uninspired. This, however, seemed to be merely a guide, and when I mentioned this working device to Lloyd, he didn't remember it.

Another phase of the motion picture comedy should be mentioned, for it is seldom realised that music played an important part in the audience's reaction to comedy. On the set music was played to fit the mood of the scene in order to stimulate the players' enactment of that scene. This use of musical accompaniment was rarely mentioned by the major comedians although Langdon indicated that he did not use the "jazz accompaniment" which was often employed on the sets where comedies were created. Instead, Langdon's interest in what is often called "pathos" prompted him to have "the sobby strains of 'Camille' " executed by the set orchestra.[63]

This practice of playing music on the set may have helped a great deal in giving pace to the performing of slapstick comedy routines and also have set the mood for the playing of serious scenes in the films. If music helped the actor, it surely improved the final product. In the Twenties all the large theatres had orchestras which used a score for the features while the smaller theatres in the towns employed a pianist. The compromise was generally the many faceted theatre organ. Today, unfortunately, film societies present the feature comic films of the Twenties without music. Some violence is done to the silent film when it is this silent even though it is projected for a special type of audience. The function of music in the Twenties was a vital one. This was brought home to me when I viewed Lloyd's *Safety Last* and *The Kid Brother* at Richard Symonton's excellent little home theatre at Tuluca Lake, California, on the evening of June 14, 1965. Gaylord Carter's organ scoring of these films had been taped and played with 16mm. prints. *Safety Last*'s climactic sequence, featuring the laboured, obstacle-packed climb up a building, was more thrilling because Carter so expertly supported the visual aspects of the film with music. Lloyd's serious moments in *The Kid Brother* were also underscored so effectively that greater emotional involvement was achieved even though we had a small group (of which Lloyd was a member) viewing the film.

Lloyd told me that he was disappointed with the attempts to render musical support for the comic film by the use of a piano. Keaton went even further. He said that he found organ music inferior to a full orchestra and desired, what might be called a purist's objection, no sound effects. When I asked him why, he replied: "That's the way it was done—with no sound effects." He then added that if he released his films in the near future, he would add only a musical score.

Chaplin can be credited with keen insight regarding the use of serious musical themes and the avoidance of the self-conscious, overdone scoring of chases and fights in his films of the Thirties, *City Lights* and *Modern Times*. The same can be said for the excellent scoring of his reissued *The Gold Rush*. Theodore Huff notes that the comedian was involved with the "scoring" of his pictures in the Twenties:

> Realising the importance of musical accompaniment to the silent film, Chaplin sought to have it reproduced in every theatre exactly as he wished it. He

supervised the cue sheets (lists of numbers to be played, sent free to all theatres booking a film) of his pictures from "The Kid" (1921) up to "City Lights," (1931)—when it was possible to have the music recorded on the film itself.[11]

It was this kind of meticulous concern that perfected the feature length comedy. Chaplin surely had his hand in the process. There was a pride in their work that made their kinds of comedy excel. Lloyd and Keaton, more than Chaplin and Langdon, were in the mainstream of creation by the middle of the Twenties. Between 1922 and 1928 Lloyd had created ten features—Keaton eleven. They were not only the most productive of the kings; they created, as perfectors of the feature length comedy, some of the best films of their careers and some of the best comedies of the twentieth century.

8. Only Four Kings

IN THE SILENT era of black and white, many comedians struggled mightily for a place in the sun beside Chaplin, Lloyd, Keaton, and Langdon. Myriads of one- and two-reel films made minor comedians' faces familiar to the moviegoer, but when the zanies were allowed to make features, they achieved only temporary recognition and, occasionally, acclaim that lasted for a span of only one or two years. If such comedians are now known by name, they are usually associated with one- and two-reel comedies.

Who, for example, can remember Billy Dooley? For a brief time he had his fling as a leading comic in one- and two-reelers. A fellow with the limber body of Ray Bolger and the face of Harry Langdon, he exhibited the acrobatic skills of a dense, child–like clown in such works as *Misfit Sailor*, a 1926 product of Education-Christie Comedies.

Some may remember Sydney Chaplin, a brother of the famous comedian, in his 1925 feature *Charley's Aunt*, a work he had presented on the stage. But who remembers his 1926 Warner Brothers Pictures *Oh! What a Nurse* and *The Better 'Ole*? In a chatty fan magazine of 1921, Sydney was considered "a rival to the world's greatest comedian"[62]—a statement which referred, of course, to his younger brother, Charles Chaplin. However, the older member of the family had only a brief season in the sun. As a supporting actor in such Chaplin masterpieces as *Shoulder Arms* (1918), Sydney displayed more than average competence, but his lack of comic invention and limited acting skill destined him to the ranks of the minor comedians—he never seriously rivalled his brother's throne.

Interest in minor comedians has been revived by the nostalgic *potpourries* concocted by Robert Youngson. By far his best conglomeration was *The Golden Age of Comedy* (1958) with less artful products like *When Comedy Was King* and *30 Years of Fun* following the initial successful work. The faces and capers of Ben Turpin, Roscoe "Fatty" Arbuckle, Charlie Chase, Harry "Snub" Pollard, Mabel Normand, Stan Laurel, Oliver Hardy, and Andy Clyde as well as three kings of the period, Chaplin, Keaton, and Langdon, have thus come alive to a generation that has been conditioned to the romantic, sexy, domestic, and sentimental comedy that is only mildly funny. While I do not believe Youngson's method of cutting and pasting sequences from one- and two-reel films to the tune of superficial narration and music always places the artistry of the comedian in the best light, he deserves praise for reviving interest in one of the greatest comedy eras of all times. He has, of course, stimulated a renewed appreciation of the minor as well as the major comedians.

One comedian that Youngson has brought to the attention of today's public is Charlie Chase, one of the comics who might have been as successful as "the big four." A prolific trouper of the comedy mills, Chase had completed many one- and two-reel works by the time sound arrived. Obviously he had a kinship with Harold Lloyd and the polite comedians. There was none of the tramp-clown in his character. Certainly there was a dash and a pleasant disposition in this laughable figure who could be easily embarrassed and frustrated. But Chase did not have that facet of will possessed by a young man striving for success that Harold Lloyd used to give his stories substance and his character distinction. Employing the trait of enthusiasm that was similar to Lloyd's handling of his character, Chase lacked the warmth and gaiety of the famous comedian's "Harold." However, I also believe Chase fell far short of Lloyd in his limited comic invention and acting skills. While the handling of his material sometimes contained a flash of originality and a flair of execution, more often he seemed to use a stock routine that Lloyd could have executed with an artful, fresh twist. Seldom did he seem to be able to employ the variations on a minor comic situation that the master of this type of comedy had perfected.

Chase's 1926 two-reel *Long Fliv the King* (which evidently was a burlesque of *Long Live the King*, a 1923 Metro production that was based on a story by Mary Roberts Rinehart) reveals some of his best acting skills. As king of a foreign country, Charlie is constantly being embarrassed before his courtiers by a plotting prime minister. This comic villain wants to provoke the king to the point of a duel for life. By alternately laughing and sneering, Chase produces a clever juxtaposition of emotions as his character is shown avoiding a display of honour without revealing his cowardice. When a duel can no longer be avoided, the comedian shows feigned daring by brandishing a sword in an unorthodox fashion that is reminiscent of Lloyd's duelling in his 1922 *Grandma's Boy* Civil War sequence.

But Chase was evidently not versatile enough to sustain his brand of comedy beyond two-reel films. Like other minor comedians of his time, he had a limited bag of tricks which were of a higher calibre than those used by the polite comedians, Charles Ray, Douglas McLean, and Johnnie Hines, but did not measure up to the seemingly bottomless bag of gags and routines which the four kings possessed.

Those patrons of the movie theatre who laughed at Youngson's *The Golden Age of Comedy* may remember the frantic capers of a mis-shapen, cross-eyed little clown with a brush moustache, Ben Turpin. Certainly one can say that he had a distinct style and a character that did not ape any one of the four major comedians. His burlesque of the heroic pose often culminated in some of the cleverest and funniest scenes in the "literature" of silent screen slapstick. His travesty of the lantern-jawed, muscular protagonist of serious films can hardly be forgotten. He was a cartoon version of the daring sheriff, the small-town hero, the dashing count. His physical appearance punctuated all his comedy—his deformed pear-shaped body, his turkey neck and white, weak-jawed face dotted with wayward eyes presented an outlandish portrait.

Turpin's comic reactions resembled Keaton's. During the chaos of a fight or in a passionate embrace of the princess, a close-up revealed his blank face and grotesque eyes. Such understatement of emotion was his forte, but he did not have the inventive genius of the "great stone face," Keaton. In fact, Turpin seemed limited to shorter works by the very cartoon nature of his bizarre character. There was a vitality, a flair in this outlandish clown that gave him a long career in short comedies and, unfortunately, a minor position and short career in features. Such an odd character had limited facets; it could hardly provide the subject of a large quantity of story material; it could only be relegated to such elaborate burlesques as his 1921 *A Small Town Idol*, a film designed to be released as a feature by Mack Sennett. A drastically cut version (from the seven reels) was reissued in 1933 with a music and soundtrack. As a two-reel work it had merit, but it did not have the quality of acting and the comic invention to sustain it as a feature length work. With a "star" packed cast, Turpin, Charlie Murray, Jimmy Finlayson, Billy Bevan, and Andy Clyde (and even Phyllis Haver, Ramon Navarro, and Marie Prevost in brief appearances) *A Small Town Idol* had the design that might indicate Mack Sennett's attempt to duplicate the successes of *Tillie's Punctured Romance* and Mabel Normand's features. But Sennett's working method did not create fully developed comedy kings. His comedy factory manufactured clown-dolls without souls. Such a puppet was Billy Bevan.

The warmth of his tramp-clown could hardly get a foothold in the one-dimension portraits which Sennett allowed him. His 1926 production of *A Sea Dog's Tale*, under the direction of Del Hanson, was an example of such a one-dimensional portrait. As the leading comic of this film, Bevan gave a performance that did not seem to have advanced from the work of comedians in the late 1910's. Nevertheless, he had an enthusiasm for his work, and his perplexed comic double-takes showed a degree of skill. Snub Pollard, a leading comedian in one- and two-reel films by Hal Roach, seems to have had similar qualities. He sometimes combined the older tradition (indicated by the overstated walrus moustache) with the new (shown by the dash of a young man trying to go places)—a mixture that was never consistent; in *Hot Off the Press* (1922), for example, his character seemed to vacillate throughout the film from the tramp figure to the eager young man. Like Sennett, Hal Roach could only assist his comedians slightly—the development of their comic abilities seemed to stop just slightly beyond that of the average comedian of the age. Pollard was a good supporting comedian for Lloyd in the late 1910's, but that seemed the limit of his talent.

Many of the minor comedians lacked the genius of an outstanding director to stimulate and control their efforts—to push them to the capacity of their comic powers. Chaplin, Lloyd, and Keaton needed only minimal guidance. They took a strong hand in every phase of creation—the story conferences, the selection of cast, the shooting of each scene, the evaluation of "rushes", the final editing, and even the promotion of their pictures. Langdon, of course, was the exception. He needed the writer-director like Frank Capra to push him to stardom. This may have been the case with such comedians as Charlie Chase, Ben Turpin, Billy Bevan, and Snub Pollard.

Only one comic phenomenon of the silent screen needs to be examined, I believe, in order to complete our study of the minor comedians—the team of Laurel and Hardy. While I cannot always share the zeal that some people display for this pair, I certainly rank their comic characters and their two-reel works during the period of 1928 and 1929 as representative of some of the best comedy of the late 1920's. By developing complicated by-play and banter between two contrasting comic characters (thus avoiding the hackneyed straightman and clown approach of vaudeville), these actors produced a unique team which created comedy unlike that employed by the big four.

Although in the eyes of a critic, the dimwitted Stan executed comedy similar to Langdon's and utilised a pantomimic skill parallel to Chaplin's in his continuance of the English music hall acting tradition*, nevertheless, he had much in his comedy that was distinctive. His character was removed from the tramp–clown strata to a slight degree and placed on the fringe of society. His friendly, Cheshire cat grin was a unique possession and a great asset to his comic portrait. Oliver Hardy was a different breed—in some ways less subtle as an actor, and less inventive. Nevertheless, he developed a character with warmth, the pretensions of a Mr. Know-It-All, and a strong attachment to a feeble-minded colleague. He created a portrait with unique, many faceted dimensions. Hardy was also skilled in presenting pretensions that disguised a pea-sized brain; his character often expressed a mild form of Edgar Kennedy exasperation at the stupidity of his partner in fortune when they confronted some obstacle. But the worm often turned when frail, wan Stan miraculously performed a feat of skill that Ollie could not fathom. The workings of Ollie's rusty mind would turn inward, and his moonface, topped with puzzled brows, would look to the camera with crestfallen confusion.

*Few people are aware that Stan Laurel was associated with Chaplin during his stage career in England and with the Fred Karno comedy troupe during its tour of the United States. See Chapter I of John McCabe's *Mr. Laurel and Mr. Hardy*, a very interesting account of Laurel's early stage work.

Confronted with problems that could be solved by a trained monkey, Stan and Ollie fumbled mightily and produced small results or ended up with chaos reigning about them. Also, they often took a minor offence seriously (as if it were a major one) and induced a crowd to engage in an orgy of physical abuse. The greatest weakness in their works lay in the development of the total film—the overall structure. The story lines, the cause and effect relationships, often went awry.

Two Tars, a 1928 classic that demonstrates the famous comedy team's use of a minor altercation which turns into an orgy of destruction, also illustrates one of the major weaknesses of a Laurel and Hardy film. Two separate parts of this two-reel movie indicate the disunity that often plagues them. The first part of the films shows Stan and Ollie engaging in a struggle with a bubble gum machine—the last part shows them provoking a fight among motorists who damage or demolish each other's automobiles. The latter portion is more ingenious, unusual, and lively. Youngson evidently realised this and used this portion in *The Golden Age of Comedy*. While there are strong variations on this theme of petty destruction by an angry mob of motorists, some repetition of gags seems to impair the overall effectiveness of the film. The strongest defect, however, is seated in the two separate parts of the work—seemingly a pasting together of two one-reel films to make a longer work.

Probably a more serious defect that cramps the effectiveness of the typical Laurel and Hardy movie and places their work several notches below the four comedy kings of the Twenties, can be illustrated by examining the lively *Liberty*, a 1929 creation. Like *Two Tars* the work does not have overall unity; it is divided into three sequences—a two-minute portion showing Stan and Ollie escaping from the police, an eight and a half minute opus with the pair trying to exchange their prisoner clothes for everyday wear, and finally, an elaborate sequence showing the duet caught on the top of the skeletal structure of an embryonic skyscraper.

The second episode is logically tied to the first, but the third has no effective link with the first two. A thin causal line features Stan and Ollie attempting to don the right pair of pants—for, in the rush to cast off their prisoner's clothes, they have grabbed the wrong pair of trousers. They cannot find a place to change, and various embarrassing situations develop as they are caught by a woman, a policeman, and several workmen in their attempt to exchange trousers. This second sequence contains a great deal of merit because the team employ a type of humour seldom used in the 1920's. A tongue-in-cheek jousting with sexual perversion or a call to answer basic bodily functions is indicated by the facial expressions of the people who discover the pair struggling with their pants. Ollie's reactions are more sensitive, and he is obviously humiliated because the whole situation is not as it appears to the onlooker. Disturbed, but deliberately slow to catch the point of the discoverers' glares, Stan alternately smiles and pouts—his face a strange burlesque of comedy and tragedy masks. This type of material was not used by Lloyd, Keaton, or Langdon. However, at times this tame Rabelaisian humour was used by Chaplin—especially in his early 1916 through 1918 two-reelers.

This second portion of the film provides excellent comedy, but the third portion reveals faults that mar the total work. This skyscraper sequence shows the team employing material that Harold Lloyd perfected and executed so artfully. Laurel and Hardy, on the other hand, do not arrange their material in a way that places the funniest and most dangerous incidents toward the climax of the sequence. The most spectacular moment shows Stan on a ladder that tilts backwards. He frantically shifts the ladder back and forth with his body weight in a way that temporarily keeps it from slipping off a narrow plank. Even though Ollie urges Stan forward, the ladder seems to have a will of its own—finally Stan falls and grasps a steel beam as the ladder falls to the street below. According to the Lloyd formula this incident should be at the very end of the episode, but it occurs two-thirds of the way through the sequence. As indicated in Chapter 4, Lloyd arranged such material in a skilful, logical form that derived the best from the situation. Laurel and Hardy have specific routines, like the incident described above, which do not have a comic "punch" for the conclusion of the incident. Lloyd has his struggling protagonist employ comic ingenuity (a thing that is comic in itself because of the perverse way the character solves a problem) or has his character meet a new, greater danger at the end of the incident. Laurel and Hardy's gags "fizzle out" at the end of the routine. (To appreciate fully the superiority of Lloyd's handling of this type of material, a person should view his 1921 *Never Weaken* and compare it with *Liberty*. If one sees his 1923 *Safety Last*, he becomes even more aware of Lloyd's artistry.)

Much stronger story lines and tighter individual scene construction exist in the works of Lloyd, Keaton, and Langdon. Even though this is a major fault in Chaplin's movies, his work is often unified by a central comic idea. Only a few of the films of Laurel and Hardy have unity; *The Music Box* (1932) and *Big Business* (1929), for example, are tightly constructed with concentration on one basic situation, conflict, and comic idea. However, these works suffer from the lack of variety. They are not comedies with the comic orchestration exhibited by the big four of the silent screen.

Furthermore, the Laurel and Hardy features of the Thirties are a degeneration from their two-reel works. The comic pair compounded their structural faults, and only an occasional effective scene revealed the same high level of comic proficiency which they exhibited in the 1928–1929 period, the era of their best work.

The comic film in general, unfortunately, suffered a sorry "sea change" with the coming of sound—for example, with *Million Dollar Legs* (1932).* This film had an excellent comedy director, Edward Cline, a man who guided Buster Keaton during his rise to fame in the early Twenties. Some of Cline's old directorial magic remained, but the new milieu had produced a metamorphosis. Sound had slowed the pace; Cline and his writers and actors seemed to be gasping for air as they tripped over words.

Symptomatically, the turkey-necked, cross-eyed Ben Turpin periodically popped up as a cloak and dagger spy in the film—a ghost, I am sure, of Silent Screen Comedy Past. He remained silent, his enigmatic face shining with clown white and his eyes eternally trying to focus on the action. He could not find a toe hold in *Million Dollar Legs*. The tramp outcast of society became the outcast of the comedy film.

Jack Oakie and his new breed of comedians, the fast talking con men, had invaded the genre. This was, of course, the type of actor that was soon to dominate the comedies of the Thirties. The glib, beaming hustler with a great deal of bounce was about to take over. Only a rare hybrid, W. C. Fields, seemed to

*While the title may sound like a Betty Grable film, it actually refers to a male runner of superhuman speed.

make the whole creative struggle worthwhile. Fields displayed a blend of two traditions—the old and the new—with his flair for both visual and verbal wit. Although he had been only moderately successful in silent pictures, his raspy, nasal voice added to his portrayal of the blustering, constantly indignant, frustrated pretender.* He was funny because the audience knew that his high-born air was a mask; his character was only one step removed from the tramp-clown. This, too, one might conclude, was symptomatic. The tramp-clown had to cover his true identity to exist in the sound film.

The tramp-clown took a back seat during the invasion of the manic humour of the Marx Brothers in such conglomerations as *Duck Soup*, created in 1933. The vaudeville team of Bert Wheeler and Robert Woolsey entered movies with *Rio Rita* (1929), based on a Broadway musical of the same name. They were mostly talk with some sight gags that followed in the silent screen tradition; of their many works in the early Thirties, *Cockeyed Cavaliers* (1934) was probably the best. The great comedians had passed their zenith by this time. Chaplin's last great film, *City Lights* (1931), while it had a soundtrack (with music and sound effects), did not attempt voiced dialogue. Essentially it was a silent film made in contempt of the barrage of words and grunts. Lloyd's *Feet First* in 1930 had moments, as did *Movie Crazy* in 1932, but the sound screen Harold had lost his dash. Keaton suffered a similar fate in

*With all his ability, Fields was never consistent in his acting skills or inventive enough in his comic routines to attain the stature of Chaplin, Lloyd, Keaton, or Langdon. Nevertheless, his *The Bank Dick* which he wrote under the outlandish pen name of Mahatma Kane Jeeves comes very near to being a classic of twentieth century comedy. In this work he appears as a ne'er-do-well named Egbert Souse who accidentally captures the robbers in the final reel of the film.

the 1929 *The Hollywood Revue* and the 1930 *Free and Easy*.

While there are many theories which try to explain why sound hurt these great comedians, the view that their skills were best suited to pantomimed action is probably most satisfactory. Voiced verbal humour was not their province, and the sound movie demanded clever dialogue. Also, it should be noted, the sound film imposed a stronger realism on these comedians. Silence had abstracted—placed the actors in a cartoon world that was removed from real life.

The special art of pantomime faded and nearly died when motion picture producers turned to the talents of the fast-talking, "stand-up" comics of vaudeville. With prolonged labour pains the sound film was born. Even though the silent screen comedy was dead, the brilliant legacy left by the four great comedians continued to influence the comic films created in the United States, England, and France. Others have tried to follow this tradition, but the best efforts have come from these three countries. And, to be sure, the influence will remain; some of the best comic films will be produced by renovating some of the techniques and materials from the silent screen.

9. Rehabilitation and Legacy

IT WOULD SEEM that the little-boy nose-thumbing of the Sennett tradition would be too tame for an age that may be fomenting a twentieth century Ben Jonson, Rabelais, or Swift. So far, this trend in the literature of the day has been a minor movement in the novel; the screen has produced the sharp, hard-hitting, but often rambling, misfiring *Dr. Strangelove* under the direction of Stanley Kubrick, with novelists Terry Southern and Peter George assisting him in the creation of a scenario. Many works have followed in its wake—so much so, that a major movement in screen comedy seems headed in the direction of "black humour." With this trend comes a revival of some of the devices of the silent screen comedy.

Following on the heels of *Dr. Strangelove* was *The Loved One*, a film with many delightful moments that parodied the pious attitudes mixed with the vigorous salesmanship of the "death merchants." While this film seemed to approach some of its incidents with the invective skill of satire, it more often moved into the realm of heavyhanded burlesque. Some influence from the silent screen tradition could be observed in some of the last broader episodes of the film when the script parted company with the novel by Evelyn Waugh that served as its model.

The Wrong Box, another "black" screen comedy, exhibits a more direct influence from the silent screen in some of its sequences—the chase episode being the most obvious. Brief portions of the film (as in the opening of *Tom Jones*) are executed in a style that mimics the old tradition. Titles, instead of spoken dialogue, and broad gestures from the actors that imitate the early screen style are employed with some effectiveness. Director Bryan Forbes utilises the seasoned acting skills of Ralph Richardson, John Mills, and Peter Sellers to help him create a gay, lively comedy that produces gravestone humour but avoids the clumsiness of *The Loved One*. He also employs the assistance of the skilled co-scenarists Larry Gelbart and Burt Shevelove who wrote the book for the 1962 Broadway musical, *A Funny Thing Happened on the Way to the Forum*.

Gallows or "sick" humour that shows the influence of the old silent screen tradition can also be seen in such Hollywood products as *Lord Love a Duck*, a poke at the beach boys and girls that sometimes lapses into an embrace; *Cat Ballou*, a burlesque of the western hero and familiar stereotypes which inhabit this world; and *What's New Pussycat?*, a conglomeration of sex and psychiatry gags chaotically woven into a *potpourri* plot by comedian-writer Woody Allen. These works have the comic, wild chases (often with accelerated motion being used) and the exaggerated fights of the older film comedy, but seem to lack the spontaneous, free charm of past works. When these present day films employ the old devices, they dampen their comedy by self-conscious execution. They often seem to engage in slapstick with the overall tone that says, "Look! Isn't this cute and clever!"

By far the most self-conscious efforts of recent years are those films that more directly ape the silent screen tradition. Abortive efforts to resurrect the comedy of the past can be seen in *It's a Mad, Mad, Mad, Mad World*, *Those Magnificent Men in Their Flying Machines*, and *The Great Race*. The first is probably the most colossal failure. A barrel full of contemporary comedians: Milton Berle, Sid Caesar, Buddy Hackett, Phil Silvers, Jonathan Winters, Terry-Thomas, etc.—plus colour and Cinerama (a cinemascope version for the provinces) could not save this epic farce from grinding away until it entered the strange valley of antic boredom. More chases, numerous comedians, a larger screen, and a longer script obviously are not criteria for making a first-rate comedy. Hollywood's uncontrolled affection for elephantiasis reveals that its producers realise (often unconsciously) that they are on shaky ground. Directors and writers of such products as *Those Magnificent Men in Their Flying*

Machines and *The Great Race* have not thoroughly investigated and absorbed some of the working methods of the great comedians of the past. They have not graduated beyond Mack Sennett's most primitive efforts to produce laughter.

Blake Edwards, director of *The Great Race*, reveals a dilettante's grasp of his task when he states, "Comedy is a science. The only way to learn a science is to study, and the only way to study is to look at what the old masters did and take from them. *Race* is an accumulation of dozens of the great comedy cliches."[76] His view betrays the fault of those who sometimes imitate an old tradition. To me comedy is more art than science; the mind and spirit (intuition, you might say) must work together—the total mood of an older tradition must be adapted to the times, and innovation must spring forth in the process of creating the work of art. Edwards and the others who follow the same path have not absorbed the spirit of this tradition—they probably don't believe in it; consequently, they poke fun at that which may already be caricatured. The comedy of Chaplin, Lloyd, Keaton, and Langdon is often rooted in burlesque. For example, the chase itself is a take-off on the elaborate, deadly serious pursuits of the straight film melodramas of the 1910's and 1920's. A burlesque of a burlesque becomes self-conscious and often artless. The old masters of comedy were not concerned with mere duplication of the clichés, as I believe my interviews with Harold Lloyd and Buster Keaton established, but were concerned with renovating and excelling with their common bag of tricks and situations. They were concerned, first of all, with the comedy character and the development of a well-motivated dramatic story that sprang from the roots of the leading comic character.

Movies akin to *The Great Race* may find a niche in film history, but I doubt that they will ever equal the works they imitate. Black humour has greater potential since it seems to fit the trend of the times; it seems to display more innovation in the use of traditional slapstick material, and it may evolve from its burlesqued treatment of the material to sound, significant satire. I don't believe it will dampen the renewed interest in the silent screen comedy; it may promote appreciation of the older tradition and bulldoze the light, "realistic" comedy into the background.

Part of the reason the silent screen comedy has been rehabilitated can be attributed to the fading of the light, romantic comedy (the Jean Arthur–Cary Grant type of vehicle) that had its heyday in the late Thirties and early Forties and the persistence of tiresome, banal, sentimental comedies (with Donna Reed or Robert Young as protagonist, for example) on television.

Despite some misguided attempts to form an elite cult of silent film comedy lovers, there has been an honest ground swell of some magnitude that has brought about the critical rehabilitation of the silent screen comedian's contribution to the world of drama and humour. Film club presentations of silent film comedies, commercial releases of comedy film anthologies, and the private film collector's fad for buying short and feature length 8mm films, have contributed to this new recognition. More books on cinema, and specifically books on the silent screen comedians, have been appearing in this last decade than before. Consequently, the comic kings of the Twenties once more have moved into the limelight. Furthermore, Keaton came out of semi-retirement (he had been a gag writer for Red Skelton movies) and presented some of his old routines and acts in some of the dramatic series on television. Both Keaton and Lloyd reissued some of their films in England and Europe where they generally received higher critical acclaim than in the

United States. Here they have sometimes been taken for granted. (The admirers of the foreign films have often failed to see the gold in their own back yard.) During an off-hour period at the Cannes Film Festival, *Harold Lloyd's World of Comedy*, a collection of sequences in the Robert Youngson's *Golden Age of Comedy* fashion, produced a standing ovation for the comedian.[4] When Lloyd's anthology was released on the market in 1962, the film received international recognition. Also, Chaplin's work has received attention from a generation that has not seen one of his major films—*Limelight* was released in 1953, and some parts of the country did not see the film because misguided patriots helped keep the work out of the movie houses. Eleven years later, in 1964, I attended a double feature, *Modern Times* and *The Great Dictator*, in New York and noticed that other Chaplin films were receiving similar revivals in this city.

The mountain of laurels heaped on Chaplin has made the restoration of Keaton, Lloyd, and Langdon particularly difficult. Admirers of Chaplin have erected a high, solid wall of praise that seems to obscure all the other comedians. These writers, it would seem, will have no other comic gods before them. During the Twenties a few critics recognised the unique qualities of these comedians and became champions of their type of comedy. For example, Robert Sherwood, a motion picture critic for the old *Life* humour magazine, who became a noted Broadway playwright, was especially impressed with Keaton and Lloyd's work and saw them as an important part of the total comic spectrum of the times. He was, of course, one of the handful of critics who had such perception.

Today, Chaplin's position has rarely been challenged and the contribution of other comedians has seldom been realised—a situation that has prompted some evaluators to overstate their praise of a comic great. Christopher Bishop, with all his sane, carefully analysed views on Keaton, has fallen into the trap that a restorer often sets for himself. He re-establishes Keaton's status in an article for the Fall 1958 *Film Quarterly*, "The Great Stone Face." In his attempt to stress Keaton's special talents he declares that the comedian possessed "the keenest and most sophisticated visual sense" of all his competitors. This generalisation is supported aptly with examples from Keaton's work, but no account is taken of his rivals' skill.* To me this is a serious oversight for I find Lloyd used the medium more effectively than Keaton; his excellent visualisation of a gag was superior. Even Chaplin had acute pictorial skill when he dealt with poignant moments in the life of the little tramp—when the lonely little fellow looked in a window at a New Year's celebration in *The Gold Rush*, and when he gazed after the departing, ornate wagons in *The Circus*. While Chaplin's visualisation is often like a theatrical tableau, it cannot be divorced from the medium; it is an antique method, but the content of such pictures burns deep in one's memory. Bishop would have a stronger case for Keaton if he had investigated Lloyd's and Chaplin's works. Keaton was not Lloyd's superior in visualisation—an equal in the best moments, maybe, but never a superior.

While I agree with many of Bishop's views on Keaton, I see in his evaluation some of the same mistakes that plague Chaplin's admirers. He finds it necessary to elevate the status of his hero by speaking of the profundities that exist in his works. This

*Rudi Blesh (in his work, *Keaton*) has a similar bias that seems to make him avoid comparisons and set forth strong claims for Keaton's innovations (which are considerable)—while overlooking the other comedy kings. He doesn't even mention Harry Langdon. He seems to be analysing Keaton's work in a vacuum.

critic tries to establish the view that Keaton's works are modern because the comedian's character, unlike others, is of our times and that he has created a comedy that reflects the essence of the machine age. And he goes much further:

> Keaton succeeded, where the surrealist films have not, in evoking a world ordered by the unconscious motives of the protagonist, a paranoid world in which objects are genuinely possessed by his contradictory impulses. Keaton's world is never rendered in the usual "dream imagery" of surrealism, but made up of the same homely backgrounds and details which Sennett had used for his own purposes. Yet Keaton's presence in these settings creates another world, with an atmosphere like that of another planet a thousand light years removed from ours, where even the light seems less direct—reflected, like lunar light, from another source.*

If one has read some of the rhapsodic writings on Chaplin's genius, one will have encountered a similar tone and mode. Such writing may reflect the private experiences of the critic who finds a great deal in the comedian, but it says little about the comic artist as an entertainer—one who makes people laugh. Granted, the comedian may unconsciously create "Man, the Fool" and thus profoundly mirror the fool in all of us, but I count such evaluations as misdirected when they claim a dimension "above" the comic to be the essence of the comedian as well as that thing which gives the creator's works to the ages.

Let me make it clear that I am essentially on Mr. Bishop's side in his desire to restore Keaton to the limelight, but I don't

*Blesh occasionally lapses into this type of evaluation, but usually remains on solid ground.

believe he needs to imply that this comedian's films will weather changing tastes better than Chaplin's by being "modern." The critic has overstepped his duty. I am content to place Keaton in the front ranks because he has produced several unique masterpieces in the Twenties (as Bishop points out in his essay) and then assign him a place within the comic spectrum—allowing for broad taste—without striving to find the best or greatest comedian.*

It is not likely that Harold Lloyd will find a critic like Christopher Bishop. His works seem too straightforward or even too transparent for elevation. James Agee gave the comedian what most Chaplin admirers would call a back-handed compliment when he wrote, "If great comedy must involve something beyond laughter, Lloyd was not a great comedian. If plain laughter is any criterion—and it is a healthy counter-balance to the other—few people have equalled him, and nobody has ever beaten him."[27]

While I'm inclined to advance the view that "plain laughter" is a comedian's main criterion for greatness and state that other criteria are secondary, I realise that a great clown has a dimension within the framework of comedy that goes beyond the run-of-the-mill laugh grabber of vaudeville, the cinema, and television. This dimension is a thing of the spirit that is hard to define; it is bound up in the character and the mere presence of the comedian. Lloyd has such a dimension—an obvious one that seems to be overlooked by critics who look for "pathos" in

*Richard Griffith and Arthur Mayer, *The Movies* (New York: Crown Publishers, Inc., 1957), follow in Bishop's footsteps but directly state that Keaton was Lloyd's superior. They make the same reduction error by linking Keaton's character to the mechanical—the understatement of emotion and companionship with machines in his films are manifestations which lead them to this conclusion.

the clown. Lloyd's comedy is infused with the spirit of Harlequin—not Pierrot. He has baskets of sunshine; he possesses a gaiety of the fullest measure that all comedians seem to possess to some degree. Without gaiety Chaplin's little tramp would be a one-sided portrait; his little fellow would merely be a wandering Sad Sack. While many critics have been impressed by the Pierrot side of Chaplin's character, they seem to overlook this spirit—a tone that is much stronger than the so-called pathos. Robert Payne's *The Great God Pan*, with all its effusiveness, relates this dimension better than the works of other critics. Furthermore, gaiety of the clown is directly linked with the spirit of comedy—the spirit of fun; and assuredly, this characteristic is possessed by all great clowns. It may be considered the essence of clowning and, obviously, that feature which makes comedy so attractive to the audience. Keaton and Langdon possessed a strong measure of this facet, but Lloyd and Chaplin surpassed them.

Since Lloyd's breezy, go-getting young man seemed to be the antithesis of Chaplin's character, he was fair game for the lovers of the Sennett tradition. In 1924 Gilbert Seldes took sharp aim:[23]

> His [Chaplin's] most notable opposite is Harold Lloyd, a man of no tenderness, of no philosophy, the embodiment of American cheek and indefatigable energy. His movements are all direct, straight; the shortest distance between two points he will transverse impudently and persistently, even if he is knocked down at the end of each trip; there is no poetry in him, his whole utterance being epigrammatic, without overtone or image. Yet once, at least, he too stepped into that lunatic Arcadia to which his

> spirit is alien; not in *Grandma's Boy*, which might just as well have been done by Charles Ray, but in *A Sailor-made Man*. Here the old frenzy fell upon him, the weakling won by guile, and instead of fighting one man he laid out a mob from behind; something excessive, topsy-turvy, riotous at last occurred in his ordered existence. He is funny; but he has no vulgarity; he is smart. He amuses me without making me laugh, and I figure him as a step toward gentility.*

Seldes, I believe, tends to overstate his case against Lloyd. I agree that the comedian is "a step toward gentility," but I do not find this "step" a grievous fault. *Grandma's Boy* done by Charles Ray would have condemned the picture to obscurity, but *Grandma's Boy* by Lloyd is quite a different thing. As I have pointed out, Keaton and Langdon (and Chaplin in *The Pilgrim*), as well as Lloyd, employed genteel comedy material. They even used such material as the basic substance of their plots. But they never embraced the tone of the genteel tradition; they held firmly to the slapstick tradition. Seldes errs when he writes that Lloyd had only one moment of frenzy. All his pictures contain sequences in which the character drops the restraints of conventional demeanour that have been a protective mask; he steals, cheats, and bowls over a policeman in a Keystone frenzy to obtain his goal. His blend of the genteel mask and slapstick aggression in his films gives him his distinctiveness. I would further state that his spirit of gaiety equals Chaplin's and gives him a "poetry" that Seldes's rather narrow taste will not allow him to embrace. In fairness to this critic, it

*This statement is from the 1957 edition and, interestingly enough, shows no alteration of viewpoint from the 1924 edition. Seldes indicates in his additions to the 1957 edition that he prefers "Keystone comedy."

should be pointed out that he was an idol breaker of sorts who was hacking away at the conventional and stuffy arts of the Twenties. He rightly saw much vitality in the "seven lively arts" —arts that were too lowbrow for people of cultivated tastes. As Seldes lashed out at the sentimental, genteel comedy, Lloyd obviously suffered because his character appeared to be solidly placed in the camp of Johnny Hines, Douglas MacLean, and Charles Ray. It is unfortunate that Seldes did not make fine distinctions.

Another common error made by critics is to overlook the importance of Lloyd's comic portrait. "Keaton, Chaplin, and Langdon were unique personalities," Joe Franklin writes. "Even if their material had been inferior, their pantomime would have put them over. But Lloyd was different—like the later sound comedians, he relied almost exclusively on his material, and it was material that could have been as effective in the hands of another comic."[48] While Franklin goes on to contradict this statement by indicating that Lloyd was the best practitioner of his material and his brand of comedy, he bases this rather confusing analysis on the frequent criticism given by others—that Lloyd was merely a good gagster—a highly skilled comic who was inventive and could string gags together with more than average finesse.

As I have indicated earlier, Lloyd's comedy depends on the integration of plot and character; a key to understanding the comic nature of his portrait lies in the young man's obsession to get ahead—his zeal magnified to a comic dimension. He becomes a ridiculous figure because he attempts feats he is ill-equipped to handle. Furthermore, some of the best comic moments in his films occur when the young man's zeal leads him to situations which backfire. For example, much against his will he is forced to assume the role of a human fly in *Safety Last*.

Another key to Lloyd's comedy will lead to the general discussion of what so many critics loosely label satire in the silent screen comedy. William Cahn, one of Lloyd's champions who has helped restore his status through his erratic, epigrammatic *Harold Lloyd's World of Comedy*, writes: "The American public welcomed Harold's hectic satire on America's young go-getter. It is improbable, at the time, that Lloyd realised he was satirising a character who had become 'the great all-American youth.' "[4] It is more likely that Lloyd *did* know what he was doing—burlesquing the go-getter that popular literature and the cinema generally treated with a seriousness close to reverence. Lloyd's autobiography, *An American Comedy*, published in 1928, and several of his earlier and later writings, many of which Cahn reproduces in his study of the comedian, indicate that he was a conscious craftsman who could express his theories on comedy and put them into practice more effectively than most comedians. Similarly, Chaplin burlesqued many serious themes in his films; *The Gold Rush*, for example, was a travesty of the rash of "he-man" adventure movies that were ground out by Hollywood in the early Twenties. In fact, Chaplin succeeded only in walking along a line between burlesque and satire until he began to take his admirers seriously. Many of these evaluators discovered satire in his Essanay and Mutual two-reelers. Chaplin probably can only be said to have achieved satire in *Monsieur Verdoux*, although I'm sure many critics will disagree with me because they define the word on a broader basis. If they do disagree, they will have to allow Lloyd this kind of "depth." But I see the spirit of the major comedians as being much broader and more carefree than the spirit of satire. Keaton and

Langdon were certainly burlesquing the heroic and romantic pose in *The General* and *The Strong Man*, with military bravery and the love of a woman being subject to some playful jostling. To me satire has a bitter edge, an invective that can be seen in the dramatic works of Aristophanes, Ben Jonson, Molière, and George Bernard Shaw. In their best moments the silent screen comedians may have approached satire, but their spirit of play was too light to cut deeply into human foibles.

In great need of a champion to restore his status in the history of motion picture comedy, Harry Langdon is as lonely an artist as he was a lonely soul on the screen.* No biography or major evaluation of his works has appeared until now; he is often mentioned as a talented comedian who gained fame under the tutelage of Frank Capra. And, it must be conceded, that is a fairly accurate statement; but, it should also be realised that both men had a genius that worked best in alliance.

Fortunately, some of Langdon's skill as a comedian can be witnessed, thanks to the preservation of two of his best films by the Museum of Modern Art Film Library. Richard Griffith, former Curator of this excellent depository, has also helped establish Langdon's importance to the silent film by essaying his talents in his discussion of Frank Capra.[49] However, James Agee was the man who could take a poet's pen to catch the many facets of this enigmatical clown:

> Chaplin and Keaton and Lloyd were all more like each other, in one important way, than Harry Lang-

*John Montgomery's *Comedy Films* devotes a chapter to both Chaplin and Lloyd, five pages to Keaton, and only one page to Langdon's work. John Howard Lawson (in *Film: The Creative Process*) sees Lloyd and Keaton as significant contributors to silent screen comedy, but he concentrates on Chaplin and slights Langdon.

> don was like any of them. Whatever else the others might be doing, they all used more or less elaborate physical comedy; Langdon showed how little of that one might use and still be a great silent-screen comedian. In his screen character he symbolised something as deeply and centrally human, though by no means as rangily so, as the Tramp. There was, of course, an immense difference in inventiveness and range of virtuosity. It seemed as if Chaplin could do literally anything, on any instrument in the orchestra. Langdon had one queerly toned, unique little reed, but out of it he could get incredible melodies.[27]

Agee also does an excellent job of describing his unique physical characteristics:

> The crown of his hat was rounded and the brim was turned up all around, like a little boy's hat, and he looked as if he wore diapers under his pants. His walk was that of a child which has just gotten sure on its feet, and his body and hands fitted that age. His face was kept pale to show off, with the simplicity of a nursery-school drawing, the bright, ignorant, gentle eyes and the little twirling mouth. He had big moon cheeks with dimples, and a Napoleonic forelock of mousy hair; the round, docile head seemed large in ratio to the cream-puff body. Twitchings of his face were signals of tiny discomforts too slowly registered by a tinier brain; quick, squirty little smiles showed his almost prehuman pleasures, his incurably premature trustfulness.

While Agee, because of the wide range of his essay, could not illustrate the facets of this clown in detail, he captured the essence of Langdon's comedy after others had failed. His only grievous error lay in repeating the questionable view that Langdon was almost as childlike as the character he portrayed.

The revival of interest in the comedy film of the silent era has not found Chaplin caught short with a lack of defenders, but once more he has been criticised for his primitive use of the motion picture medium. With the strong emphasis on slick, business-like technical production today, it is understandable that such a criticism would be revived. For example, Jack Spears seems overly harsh when he writes:

> After nearly a half-century of film-making he is still unlettered in the *mechanics* of putting a motion picture together, and he pretends to be contemptuous of what he calls "Hollywood chi-chi"—i.e., expressive camera angles and lighting, unusual pictorial composition, continuity in editing and cross-cutting. His knowledge of such directorial techniques is virtually nil.[42]

While Spears spends a great deal of space pointing out the technical inadequacies of Chaplin's work and carefully supports his thesis on the comedian's use of "collaborators" to whom he seldom gave credit, he sees Chaplin's outmoded photography and poor sets as an asset in his comedies. He objects to these weaknesses in his "serious" works—*Monsieur Verdoux* and *Limelight*.[42] Interestingly enough, Robert Payne also held the view that Chaplin's early comedies were more effective because of their crudities,[21] but he believed that Chaplin's movie skills improved. Somewhere between Spear's and Payne's viewpoints lies a more valid evaluation. Chaplin improved his technical skills slightly, but he improved his acting skills considerably. Many of the scenes of his films in the Thirties have the genius of the great, mature actor. Occasionally, his directing of others' actions was outstanding. I believe that he drew a performance from Paulette Goddard as the gamin in *Modern Times* that the actress did not equal in all her film portrayals after this initial major role. What Chaplin lacked in technical skills, he compensated for with content. And what is more important? We have many "slick" directors who grind out films with the best composition, excellent use of camera angles and lighting, and all the editing skill of Eisenstein. But they are dealers in shabby dramatic clichés.

One skill that I believe is important to the dramatic art of the comedy film was never fully developed in Chaplin's films. One major fault in his work—his inability to tell an effective, unified dramatic story—always plagued him. Chaplin's genius was scenic—episodic. He patched together a brilliant series of scenes but was weak in his handling of his overall story development. Chaplin admirers unconsciously write this off, believing that all his virtues make up for any weakness. They even go so far as to point their finger at the tightness of a Keaton or Lloyd comedy plot and accuse it of being artificial. Granted, a "well-made play" may be merely a skilfully knit mechanism, but we look for more than this in a good work. Both Lloyd and Keaton manoeuvred their works subtly along lines of a strong story development and a solid overall comic idea. At his best Chaplin used an effective central comic idea (as in *The Gold Rush*), but he invariably floundered in handling the dramatic line of his films. Such a fault is a basic artistic flaw and not merely a mechanical imperfection.

Obviously, I do not claim that the best film work which these comedians produced can be compared with the best of Aristophanes or Molière. Some rhapsodic writings on Chaplin would seem to invite such comparison. Rather than go this far, I will say that, in their own way, they represent an artistry and contain a significance which cannot be dismissed as trivial or second-rate—a very common practice by those who disparage comedy and concentrate on what they consider to be of import in serious dramatic works. Such admirers must live a one-dimensional life that cannot comprehend the total spectrum of comedy and tragedy—approaches to life that may be blended by the artist. They should be directed to such modern playwrights as Anton Chekhov, Sean O'Casey, and even Tennessee Williams. These dramatists see the total spectrum of life and often blend pathos and comedy—or, at least, place these elements in sharp juxtaposition with each other. More recently the so-called absurdists or avant-garde playwrights have concentrated on the bitter-comic side of man. The inhabitants of Samuel Beckett's *Waiting for Godot* are closely related to derelicts from a cheap, touring vaudeville show. Eugene Ionesco's one-acts and full-length plays reveal similar portraits. It is interesting to note that when these roles are performed by such talented vaudeville stars as Bert Lahr (Estragon in the Broadway production of *Waiting for Godot*), critics have lauded the enactment of the part.

Even if this significant role of comedy cannot be realised by some evaluators, one can at least conclude that the golden age of comedy in the films can be equated with the *commedia dell' arte*, a popular comedy of the Italian and French theatre three hundred years ago. This early, vital, lowly form of entertainment spawned the genius of Molière, one of the greatest playwrights of all time and an author who can be ranked with Shakespeare. Molière gleaned the plots, the comic routines, and characters of the humble humour that was executed by strolling players and blended this material with the high wit of a mannered, cultivated society. His most sophisticated works were often sprinkled with the gay slapstick of the *commedia dell' arte* tradition. From this blend he created some of the best satires of all times.

The film needs, one might say, a modern day Molière to create a higher comedy from the elements of the silent screen comedy. While I don't believe the comedy of Chaplin, Lloyd, Keaton, and Langdon needs improvement (any more than Molière needed to "improve" the *commedia dell' arte*), I believe there is some indication that the tradition of silent screen comedy need not be consigned to the same level of inferior works as those produced by the Three Stooges and the duo, Abbott and Costello. Peter Sellers and Norman Wisdom are two British comedians who have employed many facets of this old screen genre. But they are imitators, and an imitation can seldom approximate the high level of the original creation. On the other hand, the French comedian, Jacques Tati, in *Mr. Hulot's Holiday* and *My Uncle*, has come close to recapturing the comic spirit and artful humour of the Twenties. True, he does not have the economy and vigour of this tradition; his films need trimming and his progression sometimes seems laboured and self-conscious. But he has a strong sense of visual humour that jostles the foibles of our times. Like Chaplin he is a slow, discriminating creator who does not grind out features at a pace to rake in the most money in the shortest time. He writes, directs, and plays the leading role—following the same filming techniques of the big four when they were in their prime. Time will have to reveal whether or not we are on the brink of a renaissance—a modified, new age of great comedy.

Pierre Etaix, following in Tati's footsteps (he was the older comedian's gag writer before striking out on his own), has been more prominent in the promotion of this rebirth. His one-reel *Happy Anniversary* and feature work *The Suitor* (1963) show that he has studied the prototypes of the best comedy of the twentieth century. His comedy character follows the logical and steady growth that we can find in the characters created by Keaton and Lloyd. *The Suitor* displays many structural similarities to the best comic works of the Twenties. Etaix does not need the many chases, fights, and thrills that seem to fascinate the Hollywood imitators who turn out epic comedies. He has observed the "quiet moments" of the Twenties and adapted them to his style. Indeed, he, more than anyone on the contemporary scene, has adapted the tradition with skill and innovation.

One important fact remains. The *commedia dell' arte* was handed down from one family of comedians to the next. Much of its quality was on shaky ground since it depended on the proficiency of the successor. Theatre historians have only meagre records of the plays performed—brief scenarios and descriptions of actual performances. But we have the end product of silent screen comedy—the complete creation on film to pass along from generation to generation. With these films, this tradition will not die.

Bibliography

(The page numbers given after book titles are those specifically referred to in the text)

A. Main Books

1. Bardèche, Maurice and Robert Brasillach. *The History of Motion Pictures*. Translated and edited by Iris Barry. New York: W. W. Norton and Co., Inc., 1938 (pp. 24, 215, 291, 294).
2. Blesh, Rudi. *Keaton*. New York: The Macmillan Company, 1966 (pp. 67–9, 136, 137).
3. Bowman, William Dodgson. *Charlie Chaplin; His Life and Art*. London: George Routledge and Sons, Ltd., 1931.
4. Cahn, William. *Harold Lloyd's World of Comedy*. New York: Duell, Sloan, and Pearce, 1964 (pp. 98, 196).
5. Chaplin, Charles. *Charlie Chaplin's Own Story*. Indianapolis, Indiana: The Bobbs-Merrill Company, 1916.
6. ——. *My Autobiography*. New York: Simon and Schuster, 1964 (pp. 148, 150).
7. Cotes, Peter and Thelma Niklaus. *The Little Fellow; The Life and Work of Charles Spencer Chaplin*. New York: Philosophical Library, Inc., 1951 (p. 9).
8. Delluc, Louis. *Charlie Chaplin*. Translated by Hamish Miles. London: John Lane The Bodley Head, 1922 (pp. 43–4, 48–9).
9. Fowler, Gene. *Father Goose; The Story of Mack Sennett*. New York: Covici Friede Publishers, 1934 (pp. 197, 287).
10. Griffith, Richard and Arthur Mayer. *The Movies; The Sixty-Year Story of the World of Hollywood and Its*

Effect on America, From Pre-Nickelodeon Days to the Present. New York: Simon and Schuster, Inc., 1957.

11. Huff, Theodore. *Charlie Chaplin*. New York: Henry Schuman, Inc., 1951 (pp. 1, 123, 188, 226, 237).
12. Hughes, Laurence A. (ed.). *The Truth About the Movies*. Hollywood, California: Hollywood Publishers, Inc., 1924 (pp. 411, 438–441).
13. Jacobs, Lewis. *The Rise of the American Film; A Critical History*. New York: Harcourt, Brace and Company, 1939.
14. Keaton, Buster and Charles Samuels. *My Wonderful World of Slapstick*. Garden City, New York: Doubleday and Company, Inc., 1960 (pp. 94–6, 112, 134–5, 174, 207–10, 213).
15. Knight, Arthur. *The Liveliest Art*. New York: Macmillan Co., 1957 (p. 127).
16. Lahue, Kalton C. *World of Laughter*. Norman, Oklahoma: University of Oklahoma Press, 1966 (pp. 157–9).
17. Lloyd, Harold and Wesley W. Stout. *An American Comedy*, New York: Longmans, Green and Company, 1928 (pp. 57, 73, 102, 143, 145–6, 157, 171, 175).
18. McCabe, John. *Mr. Laurel and Mr. Hardy*. Garden City, New York: Doubleday and Company, Inc., 1960 (p. 213).
19. Montgomery, John. *Comedy Films*. London: George Allen and Unwin Ltd., 1954 (pp. 126, 146–7, 155).
20. O'Dell, Scott. *Representative Photoplays Analyzed*. Hollywood, California: Palmer Institute of Authorship, 1924 (p.299).
21. Payne, Robert. *The Great God Pan; A Biography of the Tramp Played by Charles Chaplin*. New York: Hermitage House, 1952 (pp. 204, 218, 281–2).

22. Seldes, Gilbert. *The Movies Come From America.* New York: Charles Scribner's Sons, 1937
23.——*The Seven Lively Arts.* 2nd Edition revised. New York: Sagamore Press, Inc., 1957 (pp. 21, 26, 29–33, 46).
24. Sennett, Mack and Cameron Shipp. *King of Comedy.* Garden City, New York: Doubleday and Company, Inc., 1954 (pp. 29, 64–5, 186, 189).
25. Sherwood, Robert. *The Best Moving Pictures of 1922-23.* Boston, Mass.: Small, Maynard and Co., 1923 (p. 11).
26. Tyler, Parker. *Chaplin; Last of the Clowns.* New York: The Vanguard Press, Inc., 1948 (p. 112).

B. Main Articles and Periodicals

27. Agee, James. "Comedy's Greatest Era," *Life* XXVII (September 5, 1949), pp. 70–88.
28. Bishop, Christopher. "The Great Stone Face" and "An Interview with Buster Keaton," *Film Quarterly*, XII (Fall 1958), pp. 10–15 and 15–22.
29. Brewster, Eugene V. "How They Make Us Laugh," *Photoplay* XXX (August 1925), pp. 40–41, 86.
30. Chaplin, Charles. "What People Laugh At," *American Magazine*, LXXXVI (November 1918), pp. 34, 134–137.
31. ——. (Interview by Richard Meryman) "Chaplin's Anatomy of Comedy," *Life* LXII (March 10, 1967), pp. 80-94.
32. Christie, Al. "What Makes You Laugh," *Photoplay* XXIX (September 1925), pp. 30–31, 125–126.
33. Friedman, Arthur B. "Interview with Harold Lloyd," *Film Quarterly*, XV (Summer 1962), pp. 7–13.

34. Herzog, Dorothy. "The Wistful Mr. Langdon," *Motion Picture Magazine*, XXXIV (October 1927), pp. 18–19, 84–85.
35. Keaton, Buster. "Why I Never Smile," *Ladies Home Journal*, XLIII (June 1926), pp. 20, 173.
36. Kennedy, John B. "It Pays to Be Sappy," *Collier's*, LXXIX (June 11, 1927), pp. 12, 28.
37. Langdon, Harry. "The Serious Side of Comedy Making," *Theatre* XLVI (December 1927), pp. 22, 78.
38. Lloyd, Harold. "The Hardships of Fun Making," *Ladies Home Journal*, XLIII (May 1926), pp. 21, 32, 50, 234.
39. Matzen, Madeleine. "That Funny Little Man," *Motion Picture Magazine*, XXXII (December 1926), pp. 36–37, 96.
40. Mullett, Mary B. "A Movie Star Who Knows What Makes You Laugh," *American Magazine*. XCIV (July 1922), pp. 36–39, 110–113.
41. Ray, Charles. "I Spent a Million to Dress Up," *Photoplay*, XXXII (September 1927), pp. 47, 131–132.
42. Spears, Jack. "Chaplin Collaborators," *Films in Review* XIII (January 1962), pp. 18–36.
43. West, Myrtle. "Our Ambrose Goes Straight," *Photoplay*, XXX (September 1926), pp. 41, 127–128.
44. Winship, Mary. "Gag Men," *Photoplay*, XXIV (July 1923), pp. 44–45, 106.

C. Further References—Books

45. Chaplin, Charles. *My Trip Abroad*. New York: Harper and Brothers, 1922 (pp. 87, 125–6).
46. Danneburg, Joseph (ed.). *Film Year Book* 1925. New York: The Film Daily, 1925 (p. 192).

47. Dressler, Marie. *The Life Story of an Ugly Duckling*. New York: Robert M. McBride and Company, 1924 (p. 128).
48. Franklin, Joe. *Classics of the Silent Screen*. New York: The Citadel Press, 1959 (p. 194).
49. Griffith, Richard. *Frank Capra* (New Index Series No. 3). London: The British Film Institute, 1950.
50. Lawson, John Howard. *Film: The Creative Process*. New York: Hill and Wang, 1964.
51. Palmer, Frederick. *Photoplay Plot Encyclopaedia*. Hollywood, Cal.: Palmer Photoplay Corporation, 1922 (p. 92).

D. Further References—Articles and Reviews

52. *Dramatic Mirror, The*. Review of *Homer Comes Home*, issue LXXXII (July 3, 1920), p. 24.
53. ——Review of *Lonesome Luke's Wild Women*, issue LXXVII (August 25, 1917), p. 21.
54. ——Review of *The Sheriff's Son*, issue LXX (April 8, 1919), p. 30.
55. *Dramatic Mirror of Motion Pictures and Stage, The*. Review of *Mickey*, issue LXXIX (August 17, 1918), p. 240.
56. *Exceptional Photoplays*. Review of *Sherlock, Jr.*, issue IV (May–June 1924), p. 2.
57. Garringer, Nelson E. "Harold Lloyd Made a Fortune by Combining Comedy and Thrills," *Films in Review*, XIII (August–September 1962), pp. 420–1.
58. *Literary Digest*. "Safety First Stuff in *Safety Last*," issue LXXVIII (July 14, 1923), p. 45.
59. Meryman, Richard. "Chaplin's Anatomy of Comedy", *Life*, LXII (March 10, 1967), pp. 80–94.

60. *Motion Picture Magazine*. Review of *The General*, issue XXXIII (May 1927), p. 60.
61. ——Review of *Tramp, Tramp, Tramp* (by Laurence Reid), issue XXXII (August 1926), p. 61.
62. *Movie Weekly*. "Rivalry in the Chaplin Family", issue of March 26, 1921, p. 23.
63. *Moving Picture World*. "*Long Pants* Promises to be Harry Langdon's Greatest Film," issue LXXXIV (January 22, 1927), p. 266.
64. *National Board of Review Magazine*. Review of *Long Pants*, issue II (April 1927), pp. 13–14.
65. *New York Dramatic Mirror, The*. Review of *Just Nuts*, issue LXXIII (April 21, 1915), p. 35.
66. ——Review of *Lonesome Luke*, issue LXXIII (June 9, 1915), p. 39.
67. *New York Times*. Review of *Long Pants*, March 29, 1927, p. 23.
68. *Photoplay*. Review of *Three's A Crowd*, XXXII (October 1927), p. 127.
69. ——Review of *Tramp, Tramp, Tramp*, XXIX (May 1926), p. 49.
70. Sennett, Mack. "The Psychology of Film Comedy," *Motion Picture Classic* (November 1918), p. 79.
71. Sherwood, Robert. Review of *The Circus*, *Life* XCI (January 26, 1928), p. 26.
72. Sobel, Bernard. Review of *Burn 'Em Up Barnes*, *Dramatic Mirror and Theatre World*, LXXXIV (September 10, 1921), p. 389.
73. ——Review of *One a Minute*, *Dramatic Mirror and Theatrical World*, LXXXIII (June 25, 1921), p. 1083.
74. *Stage*. Review of *Modern Times* (March 1937), p. 72.

75. Thomajan, P. K. "The Lafograph," *American Cinematographer*, IX (April 1928) pp. 36–37.
76. *Time*. Review of *The Great Race*, LXXXVII (September 24, 1965), p. 106.
77. *Variety*. Review of *The Gold Rush*, LXXIX (July 1, 1925), p. 32.
78. Waller, Tom. "Langdon's *Three's A Crowd* Ready on August 26th," *Moving Picture World*, XXCVII (August 13, 1927), p. 451.